The
Sephardic
TABLE

The Sephardic TABLE

The Vibrant Cooking of the Mediterranean Jews—

A Personal Collection of Recipes
from the Middle East, North Africa and India

Pamela Grau Twena

Illustrations by Sara Love

Houghton Mifflin Company

Boston New York 1998

Library of Congress Cataloging-in-Publication Data

Twena, Pamela Grau.

The Sephardic table : the vibrant cooking of the Mediterranean Jews : a personal collection
of recipes from the Middle East, North Africa, and India / Pamela Grau Twena ; illustrations by
Sara Love.

p. cm.

Includes index.

ISBN 0-395-89260-0

1. Cookery, Sephardic. I. Title.

TX724.T84 1998

641.5'676—dc21   98-14216

Designed by Susan McClellan and Eugenie Delaney

Front cover illustration by Sara Love

Printed in Canada

BB 10 9 8 7 6 5 4 3 2 1

This book is dedicated to my mothers
Mary Grau, my inspiration
Claire Twena, my teacher
Ann Grau, my friend

Acknowledgments

AS WITH ANY PROJECT, numerous people have been supportive and helpful. I want to thank all the women who so graciously allowed me into their kitchens and shared their lives and culinary insights with me. I also want to thank my dear friends Nicole and Jaco Halfon, Evelyne Guez, Donna and Serge Cohen, Danielle Zagha, Annette Cohen and Michael Many, who were all part of my original book project and have continued to support my vision. Thank you to all of Yacov's family, the Twenas and the Kamaras, in all four corners of the world, who have fed me with love and generosity and given me an insider's view of cultures I did not know previously. Thanks to my father, Mel Grau, a wonderful storyteller, and my sister, Claudia, who mirrors my spontaneity. Thank you to my friend Erica Taylor, who carefully read my words before I sent them out to my editor. Thank you to Jane Dystel for being my agent and to Rux Martin of Houghton Mifflin Company for taking the chance and for stretching my vision. The greatest thanks go to my family: my husband, Yacov, and our children, Satya, Jonathan and Claire, who have patiently allowed me the time and space to write this book.

In many ways, this book is the by-product of the important women in my life, the first being my mother, Mary Grau. She was a great cook and visionary, and she gave me a thirst for knowledge, a gypsy spirit and a knack for creativity. My mother-in-law, Claire Twena, taught me about service, generosity and devotion. Finally, Ann Grau, my stepmother, my dear fan and friend, is holding me accountable for all measurements and cooking times. I love you all.

Contents

Introduction

MY INTRODUCTION TO SEPHARDIC COOKING, the cuisine of Jews with ancient roots in Spain, began in 1981. I had recently met Yacov, the man who would become my husband, in a star-crossed, swept-off-my-feet, full-blown-collision blind date, and within weeks of our meeting I found myself in Israel facing a life and culture for which I had no reference. We had spontaneously jetted off to Israel to attend the wedding of Yacov's brother, Ezra. Minutes after arriving in Jerusalem, I was offered an array of foreign food: pickled pink turnip slices; pastries filled with chickpeas, cumin and onions; and rice with chicken heavily laced with cardamom and allspice—all in a setting that was unfamiliar

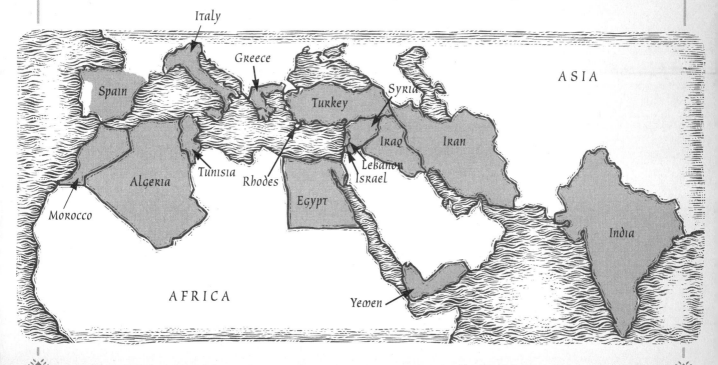

to me. Little did I suspect that Claire Twena, the exotic Iraqi mother of my handsome Yacov, was to change my culinary life forever.

I had grown up in an assimilated Hollywood family, where trendiness was enlarged to screen-sized proportions. The only culinary rules I remember from my parents' home were that we did not eat Chinese food two days in a row and that cookies could be eaten for breakfast if they were oatmeal. My own family had little knowledge of its Jewish background. We were second- and third-generation Americans. My grandmother's matzo ball soup, semi-annual brisket and occasional cheese blintzes were our only links to an ancient and noble past. It was difficult for me to comprehend a way of life where tradition ruled even the smallest gesture in the kitchen. In the Twenas' home, everything had significance: the direction sauces were stirred in, the cutlery one used for various dishes, the blessings recited over every meal—all actions were connected to the practice of piety.

I F I WAS SURPRISED BY MY NEW ORTHODOX PARENTS-IN-LAW, it was second to the alarm they must have experienced upon meeting me. They were a respected Iraqi Jewish family that could trace flawless roots back many generations. They had immigrated to Palestine from Iraq in the 1930s, with the belief in the future of a Jewish state. Their family had always married with other Iraqi families, and the marriages were usually made by arrangement. So when I arrived in Israel, passionately involved with their son, whom I had just met in Santa Monica, California, they were not sure what to do. I was religiously ignorant, was a recent graduate of a liberal women's college pursuing a career as a painter and towered 5'7" in bare feet over my mother-in-law's stout 4'11" frame. We had much ground to conquer.

Yacov and I created a home and life in Los Angeles. We took annual trips to Israel and enjoyed extended visits from his parents after the birth of each of our children. Over time, my knowledge and understanding of the Iraqi Jewish culture expanded. But the real change came in 1987 when my husband and I took a sabbatical in Israel. Our plans had included a brief stay with his parents until we found a place of our own, but as it happened, Yacov's parents would not have us live anywhere else. Their home became ours.

As with any mother- and daughter-in-law relationship, it took some time for Claire Twena and me to bond. We had a language barrier—Claire spoke Arabic and Hebrew, and I spoke only English and college French. We came from different worlds. Yet we were committed to finding something other than our love for her son to bind us. The link came with my sincere interest in her way of cooking.

FOOD HAD ALWAYS BEEN a love of mine, and I was mystified by the endless stream of dishes that seemed to materialize effortlessly behind Claire's closed kitchen door. The food she served humbled my taste buds. Spices such as cardamom, allspice and nutmeg, which she used to season chicken and meat dishes, were new to me. Claire orchestrated combinations of sweet and sour, pungent and mild, with the precision of a conductor. She also understood how to use contrasts in cooking, how to balance a dish with opposing flavors as well as colors. She added spices with varying intensities. In fact, one of my first Hebrew words was *hariff*, which means spicy. I quickly learned how to pose it as a question before tasting a dish and also how to reply when she looked into my startled face and asked me whether a particular dish was beyond my level of tolerance. My esteem for her grew as I recognized her artistry and realized that cooking was the only medium of expression available to women of her culture. I learned to appreciate the superstitions attached to seemingly everything. When she baked, she pinched off a small piece of dough and threw it away as a protection against the evil eye. But the bread itself was a different thing: it must never be tossed out. It could be turned into crumbs, bread salad or bread pudding or fed to the birds, but it could not be thrown into the garbage.

I would like to say that Claire was as impressed by my eagerness to learn as I was by her skill, but that was not quite the way it was. She enjoyed having such an appreciative fan, but she was comfortable in her role as the family matriarch. It was many months before she finally allowed me into the kitchen to watch and ask questions. Even then, instruction came in small portions. I felt like a guru's disciple, gaining enlightenment in morsels. As it turned out, not only did Claire teach me some of the dishes that had been handed down from generations before, but she also gave me insight into the essential ingredients of the Sephardic kitchen: a generous soul and a serving heart.

CLAIRE'S COOKING was not an arbitrary act of deciding what she felt like eating that night: there were unspoken rules that everyone in her community seemed to understand. Food had its own rules and rhythm. For example, one should not serve black olives on Shabbat because they are reserved for sorrow or common meals; only green olives are appropriate. One should not have dairy meals on Friday night because the Shabbat meal must be "fit for a king"; meat and chicken are considered more appropriate to the occasion. (The laws of Kashrut—kosher—prohibit mixing dairy and meat dishes in the same meal.) Certain foods are reserved for special holidays or seasons. Vegetables and fruits have symbolic meanings attached to them. But even more curious to me than these rules was the fact that all the Iraqi mothers I met seemed to do things the same way in the kitchen. They made the same type of stuffed chicken, *t'bit*, a slowly roasted bird stuffed with cardamom, allspice, rose petals and rice, for Shabbat afternoon, and they prepared most of their other foods in the same traditional manner. Nothing was random.

Up to the point when I met my husband, my own life had been a shining example of free choice, and learning the concept of Kashrut was one of the most challenging things I have ever done. One must be constantly aware of dietary laws. Only animals that chew their cud and have cloven feet, usually tamed or passive animals, such as cows, sheep and goats, are permitted as food. Camels, horses, rabbits, cats, dogs and pigs are out—no problem! Most birds are OK. Fishes must have fins and scales—no sharks or swordfish and no shellfish, crustaceans or eels. This requires analytical thinking. One cannot eat anything with blood or diseases or injured body parts, which means that the meat and fowl must pass the inspection of an authorized rabbinical butcher and the meat or fowl must have been killed in a humane manner by a *shohet* (a slaughterer who is pious and learned). The hardest prohibition for me was not mixing meat and dairy in the same dish or in the same meal. Because of this restriction, one cannot serve food containing cheese, milk or butter on plates that were used to serve meat or fowl. (Fish is pareve, which means neutral, though it sometimes has its own fork and plate.) Two sets of dishes and utensils are required. Different pots and pans for the preparation of the food, different table linens and, in many cases, different sinks in the kitchen are necessary. G-d forbid that you mix something up—the pot or fork must be buried, burned or boiled. To one born and raised in the Jewish tradition, all of these rules seem second nature, but for me, it was a cross between playing a complicated game and being on a very long diet.

IN ADDITION to the challenge of keeping kosher, there was the observance of Shabbat, the day of rest, the pinnacle of the week and the most important holiday. In the beginning, I assumed that Shabbat would be easy to observe: I could knit and watch TV and maybe clean my closet. But no, there were walks to the synagogue and long elaborate lunches, followed by naps and late-afternoon tea with friends. In most biblical interpretations, one cannot create or change things on Shabbat, which begins 20 minutes before sunset on Friday night and ends after the appearance of three stars on Saturday night. This definition of rest means that one cannot turn on a light, ignite a stove, turn on a television or stereo or drive a car. Nor can one sew, draw, paint, write or have a financial transaction—the list goes on.

People have devised ingenious ways of functioning while staying within the ground rules of Shabbat. In the kitchen, electrical devices are put on timers, and food is prepared ahead of time and kept warm in slow-cooking ovens or crockpots. The restrictions have developed dishes that are intrinsically Jewish: *d'finas*, *t'finas*, *scheenas*, *hameems* and *cholents*, long-cooking meals that generally contain meats, grains, potatoes, vegetables and eggs roasted in their own shells. These dishes provide a warm meal for Shabbat afternoon and are served with pride. It was difficult for me to hurry up to rest, but I soon found that hectic weekdays melted into a special kind of day, where time passed by on a different clock. It was like a Thanksgiving or New Year's Day that came every week.

The ritual of cooking for Shabbat began on Thursday morning at daybreak with the clanging of pots and pans and the whoosh of running water emanating from the kitchen. Food that had been purchased on Wednesday, market day, was washed, peeled and salted. By

Thursday afternoon, the kitchen was filled with steam and wonderful aromas. On Thursday night, a simple dairy meal called *kitchree* was served as a contrast to the elaborate meal on Friday night. *Kitchree* is a traditional Iraqi dish made with a fragrant mixture of rice, red lentils, cumin, garlic and butter and is served with yogurt. On Friday, the house was cleaned from top to bottom. One could tell from the street that it was Friday, because carpets hung over the balconies and the smell of household cleaners filled the alleys. By late afternoon Friday, the house was in order and the table was set with a white tablecloth and the finest tableware. Customarily, fresh flowers were brought home by a family member or a visiting guest, and the house had the feeling of anticipation. Just before sunset, candles were lit and blessed. Then the women drank tea and chatted while waiting for the men to return from the synagogue. Prayers were recited, the bread and wine were blessed, hands were ceremoniously washed, and eating soon began. The family remained together eating, talking, walking, praying, reading and playing games until the following evening. For me, just remaining in the same room with one's family for so many hours was a novel notion. Later, I discovered that this celebration was not exclusive to the Iraqi clan of which I had become a part but was common to many other Jewish families across the world.

It is a simple yet colorful existence in which meals are enjoyed and elevated to moments of importance and where every occasion is an opportunity to feast. Characterized by the use of communal serving platters and an abundance of food, these festive meals always begin with a *mezze* course, which is an array of marinated salads and appetizer dishes. Then, just when you are sure the dinner is over, the main meal begins. For a Shabbat meal, a fish course and chicken, beef or lamb are served. The meal ends with a variety of cookies, cakes, dried fruits and nuts served with Turkish coffee or tea. Abundance is an important element of every traditional Sephardic meal. "If there are no leftovers, you did not make enough," one woman told me.

Hugette Galante, a Syrian woman who shared many Syrian and Lebanese dishes with me, told me that her children had always asked her for her recipes and that somehow there was never enough time. This was a common sentiment among the women I cooked with or interviewed—they did not know how to pass on their way of life; the pace had changed. I felt that if the recipes were to be recorded, now was the time. I began by interviewing Yacov's extended family and then friends and their families, but after asking a Yemenite taxi driver in Israel about his favorite cuisine and suddenly finding myself in his mother's kitchen, I realized that I was interviewing everyone Sephardic. The process of asking questions and collecting recipes became a passion. After returning to Los Angeles in 1988, I met many other Sephardic women, mothers of my children's friends at a Sephardic day school: Jewish immigrants to California from North Africa, Greece, Turkey and the Middle East.

Although I could often persuade Sephardic women to part with recipes they'd refused to give their own daughters, pinning them down on measurements was difficult. Sephardic cooks never measure. Sometimes a measuring cup meant a Turkish coffee cup or several handfuls, sometimes a pinch meant three tablespoons, and no one ever mentioned salt, which was added in varying degrees. When I asked how many eggs were to be used in a dish, one woman replied indignantly, "How can I tell you? It depends on the chickens that day, it depends on the freshness of the flour!" This cook, who had never read a cookbook or attended a cooking class, could sense the density of an egg yolk by holding it in her palm.

What had begun as a few recipes from my mother-in-law evolved into a collection that became a forum for my Sephardic friends to share their recipes with one another. Soon I realized that the recipes were also being seized upon by people who were not Jewish. And no wonder: Sephardic recipes have an intriguing array of spice combinations, they feature many vibrant vegetarian dishes, and they are healthful and practical. Best of all, one does not have to be a great cook to produce a delicious meal.

The resulting work is a cookbook or a scrapbook that provides a glimpse into the ancient art of Sephardic cooking. It is my hope that my own personal journey will inspire readers to create with their own hands and hearts the cuisine that has a past in distant and exotic lands.

The Sephardic Jews

THE TERM "SEPHARDIC JEWS" encompasses two groups. The first is those Jews who were forced out of Spain during the Inquisition and the Jewish expulsion of 1492. The second group consists of Jewish communities that lived within the Middle East, generally under Islamic rather than Christian rule, and that followed the Babylonian Talmud. Also included in the term are Jews from Iraq, Syria, Iran, Lebanon, Yemen and India—communities that were not really affected by the Spanish refugees.

The "Golden Years" of Spanish Jewry extended from the eighth century through the fourteenth. During those years, Jews emerged as physicians, statesmen, merchants, artisans and philosophers contributing to the strength and dimensions of the Spanish Empire. They were educated, affluent and proud. Except for the ongoing threat of forced conversion to Christianity and political upheavals, these Jews were, for the most part, a stable society within Spain. Many found it easier to convert to Christianity publicly while maintaining secret Jewish lives within their homes. These Jews were called *Nuevos Christianos* or *Marranos*.

But the marriage of Ferdinand of Aragon and Isabella of Castile in 1480 altered the course of history forever. The two monarchs decreed that Spain would have one king, one law and one faith, a decision that ultimately led to the Edict of Expulsion for all Jews in 1492. Jews were given the choice of converting and dealing with the Inquisition tribunals or of liquidating all that they had within four months and leaving Spain. Census numbers tell the story: 190,000 to 250,000 Jews left Spain in 1492. The exiles called themselves *Sephardim*, from the word *Sepharad*, Hebrew for Spain.

At the time of the Spanish expulsion, the Ottoman Empire was the most powerful kingdom in the world. Its territories included what later became Turkey, Greece, Rhodes, Tunisia, the Balkans, Yugoslavia, Romania, Bulgaria, much of the Middle East, parts of Austria,

Egypt and Palestine. The empire began with Sultan Mehmet II, who, after successfully conquering the Byzantine stronghold of Constantinople in 1453, decided to transplant the Jews already existing within his borders to help rebuild his new city. Knowing that these Jews had powerful commercial trade connections throughout the world, he offered them his personal assurance for their security, a concept previously unknown in the Jewish world.

In 1481, when Bayezid II took control of the Ottoman throne, he continued the protection of the Jewish population. Upon hearing of the Edict of Expulsion, he sent out an invitation for Jews to settle in the Ottoman Empire. Referring to King Ferdinand, Bayezid II allegedly asked, "Can you call such a king wise? He is impoverishing his country and enriching my kingdom." It is estimated that 90,000 Jews arrived in Turkey in 1492. In the same year, others fled to Morocco (40,000 arrived in Fez), France (10,000), Italy (10,000), Amsterdam (25,000) and North and South America (5,000); many relocated to Portugal, only to be expelled a year later.

Often these Jews did not mix with the existing Jewish population, preferring to establish their own synagogues and learning centers. In many cases, the indigenous Jewish communities were absorbed into the newer Sephardic culture. The Sephardic communities remained bonded to one another by a language called Ladino, a mixture of Hebrew, Castilian Spanish and sometimes Arabic. Even 500 years later, they continued to pass on the language, traditions and memories of their lost glory as they also absorbed the flavors of their new countries.

During the last century, Sephardic communities in the world have gone through significant changes. Not since the expulsion from Spain have so many Jewish families changed their homelands. Although the international Jewish community has been in flux throughout history, even more dramatic shifts have occurred in the last 50 years. Persecution brought about the disbanding of the ancient communities in the Mediterranean and Middle Eastern countries, and World War II took a further toll on the populations. Later, the creation of the state of Israel brought on an anti-Jewish reaction in the Arab world that caused the communities to relocate. The world has changed, and no one is going home. The food and cultures that were so treasured and closely preserved will never be quite the same again. Gradually, the flavors and colors of the Sephardic world are being absorbed into the new melting pot of the Jewish people.

Mezze

(Appetizers)

Recipes

✴

MOROCCO
Moroccan Carrot Salad

THE FIRST TIME I TASTED THIS SALAD, I was in Israel—somewhere between Be'ersheba and Eilat. I was with my husband in the middle of the desert, in sweltering heat with a broken-down car. My enthusiasm was declining as my blood pressure climbed. We found a little roadside café and stopped for a black beer while our car was being repaired. We were served many exotic salads, but this one was the most delightful. The marinade of cumin, olive oil, lemon, garlic and salt is called a *charmoula*. It is a typical Moroccan dressing.

1 pound carrots	½ teaspoon cumin
3 tablespoons lemon juice	¼ cup finely chopped fresh cilantro
2 tablespoons olive oil	or Italian parsley
½ teaspoon paprika	Salt and pepper
2 garlic cloves, chopped	

Peel and wash the carrots. Bring a large pot of salted water to a boil. Add the carrots and cook until crisp-tender, approximately 15 minutes. Rinse under cold water. Let cool and slice into rounds.

Whisk together the lemon juice, oil, paprika, garlic and cumin in a small bowl. Pour the dressing over the carrots and mix gently. Add the cilantro or parsley and season to taste with salt and pepper. Mix thoroughly. Serve chilled.

Serves 6.

Tomato and Pepper Salad

 THIS RECIPE FOR STEWED TOMATOES with roasted peppers requires some patience, but it is well worth it. It's important to thoroughly cook the liquid out of the tomatoes, which can take a bit of time, depending on their moisture. I occasionally use stewed tomatoes from a can to hurry up the process, but I prefer fresh ones.

Forget what this salad looks like! Scoop some onto a piece of bread and experience the sublime.

5 pounds tomatoes	2 hot red peppers, seeded and
2 pounds green peppers,	chopped (optional)
pricked with a fork	1 teaspoon paprika
¼ cup olive oil	Pinch of cayenne pepper
5 garlic cloves, minced	

To peel the tomatoes, begin by cutting an X in the base of each one. Drop the tomatoes into a pot of lightly salted boiling water and boil for just 1 minute, or until the skin puckers slightly. Remove immediately, rinse under cold water and set aside in a colander. The outer skin should now peel off easily. Squeeze the tomatoes to remove the seeds and then cut the tomatoes into chunks. Set aside.

Preheat the broiler, with a rack about 5 inches from the heat. Place the green peppers under the broiler and broil on all sides until the skin is charred and becomes loose. Set aside, covered with foil, until cool enough to handle. Peel off the charred skin and remove the seeds. Cut the peppers into strips.

In a large pot, heat the oil, add the garlic and sauté for 2 to 3 minutes, or until softened. Add the tomatoes and simmer, stirring as needed to avoid burning. Continue cooking until most of the liquid has evaporated. Add the peppers (including the chopped hot peppers, if using) and spices. Continue simmering for 1 hour more, or until all the liquid is gone.

Transfer to a medium bowl and serve warm or chilled.

Serves 10 to 12.

Grilled Pepper Salad

GRILLED MARINATED VEGETABLE SALADS have recently become so popular in the United States that one could easily believe that they are a new concept in cooking. Actually, however, they have been around for thousands of years in the Mediterranean and the Middle East. Originally, before refrigeration, cooking and marinating vegetables served to extend their life span and preserve their color. Now people love these salads for their heightened flavor. This one can be made with a variety of vegetables: cauliflower, zucchini, mushrooms, green beans or eggplants. The vegetables can be sautéed, roasted or steamed before being marinated. Serve with bread.

2 pounds green peppers, pricked with a fork	Juice from 1 lemon
1 hot green pepper (optional)	5 garlic cloves, minced
¼ cup olive oil	Salt and white pepper

Preheat the broiler, with a rack about 5 inches from the heat. Broil the peppers (including the hot pepper, if using), turning until the skin is slightly charred and becomes loose. Set aside, covered with foil, until cool enough to handle. Peel off the charred skin and remove the seeds. Cut the peppers into thin strips and place in a medium bowl. In a small bowl, whisk together the olive oil, lemon juice, garlic and salt and pepper to taste. Pour the dressing over the peppers and mix gently. Adjust the seasonings. Serve at room temperature or chilled.

Serves 4 to 6.

TURKEY
Eggplant and Pepper Salad

THE "GOLDEN YEARS" OF SPANISH JEWRY were cultivated under the influence of Syrian tastes. When the invaders who came from Syria settled in Spain during the eighth century C.E., they imported the flavors from their homeland, shipping fruit trees, grains, spices and vegetables, including eggplant. This eggplant and pepper salad is a Middle Eastern classic.

2 medium eggplants, skin pierced on each side with a knife	½ cup finely chopped fresh parsley
1 green pepper, skin pierced on each side with a knife	3 garlic cloves, finely chopped
	2 green onions, finely chopped
1 sweet red pepper, skin pierced on each side with a knife	Juice from 1 lemon
	3 tablespoons extra-virgin olive oil
	Salt and pepper

Preheat the broiler, with a rack about 5 inches from the heat. Place the eggplants and peppers under the broiler and broil, turning several times, until the skin is slightly charred and becomes loose. Set aside, covered with foil, until cool enough to handle. Peel the peppers, put them in a colander and allow the juices to drain. Peel the eggplants. In a medium bowl, mash the eggplant pulp with a fork. Slice the peppers and add them to the bowl. Mix in the parsley, garlic, green onions, lemon juice and olive oil. Season to taste with salt and pepper. Chill, then bring to room temperature for serving.

Serves 6.

Iraq
Fried Eggplant Salad

DURING ONE OF THE FIRST TRADITIONAL IRAQI SHABBAT BRUNCHES I shared with my new family in Israel, my mother-in-law passed me a platter of darkly fried eggplant slices, followed by an array of salads, a dish of black-eyed peas, deep brown eggs and a bowl of curdled cream. I turned to my husband with an expression of horror. Did they really expect me to eat this so early in the morning? Yes, they did, and I was expected to love it.

Actually, I do enjoy this fried eggplant dish, and I make it often, though not before lunch. The fried eggplant slices can be presented on a platter the minute they are fried, or they can be served as a marinated side dish, as in the recipe given here.

2 large eggplants	Juice from 2 lemons
Kosher salt	2 garlic cloves, minced
Vegetable oil for frying	

Cut the dark outer skin off the eggplants. Slice them into rounds ½ inch thick. Put the slices in a colander and sprinkle with salt. Let stand for at least 30 minutes. Moisture will begin to form on the surface of the slices, and the eggplant should be pliable. Squeeze each slice dry.

Pour about 1 inch of oil into a large deep skillet. Heat the oil, and when it is hot, add the eggplant slices. Do not crowd them; fry in batches, adding more oil if necessary. Turn the slices once and fry until each side is dark brown (not burned but darker than golden). Remove with a slotted spoon. Drain on paper towels.

In a small bowl, mix together the lemon juice and garlic.

Place the eggplant slices in a medium bowl and pour the lemon juice mixture over them. Marinate for at least 1 hour. Serve chilled or at room temperature.

Serves 4 to 6.

MOROCCO
Moroccan Eggplant Salad

NICOLE HALFON, who was born in Morocco and now lives in Los Angeles, slowly roasts eggplants over the gas flame of her stove, which produces the subtle charred flavor that is so good in this dish. It is also possible—and easier—to broil the eggplants, but the results of flame-roasting are superior if you have the time.

2	large eggplants, pricked with a fork	½	teaspoon salt
2	garlic cloves, mashed	2	tablespoons olive oil
2	tablespoons minced fresh cilantro		Juice from 1 lemon
½	teaspoon paprika		

To roast the eggplants over a flame, attach them one at a time to a long-pronged fork with a wood-covered handle. Hold the eggplant over an open gas flame, 1 to 2 inches above the flame, turning to roast on all sides. The skin should be dark and slightly brittle but not black. Alternatively, if you are planning to broil the eggplants, place them on a baking sheet and preheat the broiler with a rack about 5 inches from the heat. Broil the eggplants until tender, about 15 to 20 minutes, or until the outer skin becomes charred. Peel the eggplants and drain the pulp in a colander. Using a fork, mash the eggplant pulp with the garlic and cilantro in a medium bowl. Add the paprika and salt. Heat the oil in a large skillet, add the eggplant mixture and sauté over medium-high heat until the oil is absorbed.

When the eggplant mixture has cooled, transfer to a serving plate and sprinkle with lemon juice. Serve at room temperature.

Serves 4 to 6.

IRAQ
Cooked Vegetable Salad

HE DIRECTIONS FOR THIS SALAD were given to me by an elderly Iraqi woman on a park bench in Israel. As she enthusiastically described the measurements with her ancient hands, I scribbled down what I heard and approximated the pinches and handfuls into cups and teaspoons. The results delight my family and guests.

1 large eggplant, peeled and chopped into 1-inch cubes	2 cups peeled, seeded and coarsely chopped tomatoes
Salt	¼ cup chopped green onions
¼ cup olive oil for frying	¼ cup chopped fresh parsley
2 cups coarsely chopped green pepper	¼ cup lemon juice
	1 teaspoon pepper

Sprinkle the eggplant cubes with salt and let stand for 10 minutes, then squeeze out the bitter juices. Rinse and pat dry.

Heat the oil in a large skillet, add the eggplant cubes and sauté until golden, about 10 minutes. Transfer with a slotted spoon to a mixing bowl. Sauté the green pepper in the skillet until soft, about 5 minutes. Transfer to the mixing bowl. Add the tomatoes to the skillet and sauté until the juices evaporate, then transfer to the bowl. Let cool. Add the green onions, parsley and lemon juice. Sprinkle with 1 teaspoon salt and the pepper and mix well. Refrigerate for at least 1 hour. Serve chilled.

Serves 4 to 6.

GREECE/TURKEY

Greek (or Turkish) Salad

THIS SALAD IS NOT THE TRADITIONAL "GREEK SALAD" with feta cheese. The vegetables are finely diced. In Israel, dicing salad vegetables into the smallest pieces is an art.

4 large tomatoes, diced	½ cup minced fresh parsley
1 cucumber, peeled and diced	Juice from 1 lemon
4 green onions or 1 red onion, minced	¼ cup olive oil
½ cup chopped black olives (preferably kalamata or other Greek variety)	1 teaspoon salt
	Dash of pepper

Combine the tomatoes, cucumber, onion, olives and parsley in a medium bowl. In a small bowl, whisk together the lemon juice, oil, salt and pepper. Pour the dressing onto the vegetables. Let marinate for 10 minutes. Serve chilled.

Serves 4.

ALGERIA
Chickpea Salad

THIS ALGERIAN SALAD—chickpeas marinated in a basic dressing—is an example of how simple a *mezze* dish can be. If you wish to start with dried chickpeas, first soak them overnight in double the amount of water (¾ cup dried chickpeas will yield about 2 cups cooked). Drain the chickpeas, then cook them in 2 cups water in a saucepan by bringing to a boil, covering and simmering until tender, 1 to 2 hours, adding ¼ teaspoon salt midway through the cooking. Drain again, and the chickpeas are ready to use.

6 tablespoons olive oil	2 cups canned or home-cooked
3 tablespoons red wine vinegar	chickpeas (garbanzo beans)
¾ cup finely chopped fresh parsley	1 medium onion, finely chopped
Salt and pepper to taste	

Mix together the oil, vinegar, parsley and salt and pepper in a small bowl. Rinse the chickpeas well and place them in a medium bowl. Add the onion and dressing and toss gently. Let stand at least 1 hour so that the chickpeas absorb the flavors of the dressing. Serve chilled.

S e r v e s   4 .

Turkish Mushroom Salad

ONE OF THE MANY FAUX PAS I HAVE MADE in the Middle East was to eat the *mezze* portion of the meal assuming it was dinner. This is not hard to do because this course sometimes spans several hours. When you are finally served the main meal, you must consume it with great enthusiasm, or your hosts will be offended.

The following recipe is one of the simplest *mezzes* and so delicious that it can easily prompt guests to go overboard. One can substitute steamed cauliflower, green beans or an assortment of other fresh or steamed vegetables for the mushrooms. The vegetables should be cooked al dente.

1 pound small fresh button mushrooms, whole or sliced, washed and patted dry	1 teaspoon dried thyme Juice from ½ lemon
4 tablespoons olive oil	½ teaspoon salt
2 garlic cloves, crushed	¼ teaspoon pepper
5 tablespoons finely chopped fresh parsley	*Harissa* (hot pepper sauce) to taste (optional)

Sauté the mushrooms in the oil in a large skillet over medium heat until golden, about 5 to 10 minutes. Add the garlic, parsley and thyme and continue to cook for 2 to 3 minutes more. Remove the skillet from the heat. Stir in the lemon juice and season with salt, pepper and *harissa*, if using. The dish can be refrigerated for up to 2 days. Serve cold or at room temperature.

Serves 4 to 6.

TUNISIA
GILDA'S SALAD

WHEN WASHING AND PREPARING HER VEGETABLES for couscous, my friend Evelyne Guez separates them into those that will be cooked in the broth and those that will be eaten raw as a marinated salad. Cut the vegetables into uniform ¼-to-½-inch pieces.

½ cup chopped celery	3 tablespoons lemon juice
½ cup chopped fennel	3 tablespoons extra-virgin olive oil
½ cup peeled, chopped turnip	Salt and pepper
½ cup chopped zucchini	*Harissa* (hot pepper sauce)
½ cup chopped tomatoes	to taste (optional)
¼ cup finely chopped fresh cilantro or mint	

Combine all the chopped vegetables and the cilantro or mint in a glass or ceramic bowl. Whisk together the lemon juice and olive oil in a small bowl and add salt and pepper to taste and *harissa*, if using. Refrigerate for several hours so that the vegetables absorb the flavors. Serve chilled or at room temperature.

SERVES 4 TO 6.

TUNISIA
Turnip Salad

RAW TURNIPS HAVE A PUNGENT TASTE, yet after they are salted and dressed with seasonings, they become mild. The important thing is to slice the turnips very thin and to squeeze out all the juices after salting. Adjust the amount of *harissa* to your own palate.

2 small young turnips, peeled (leaving a little of the purple base on for color) and thinly sliced	2 tablespoons lemon juice
Salt	½ teaspoon *harissa* (hot pepper sauce)
1 orange, peeled and cut into small pieces	1 small garlic clove, minced
	3 tablespoons olive oil
	Pinch of caraway seeds

Sprinkle the turnips with salt and set aside for 1 hour, then squeeze out the excess liquid. In a medium bowl, combine the pieces of orange, lemon juice, *harissa* and garlic. Add the turnips to the mixture and combine. Stir in the olive oil and caraway seeds. Refrigerate for at least 2 hours or overnight. If desired, add more *harissa* for a spicier flavor. Serve chilled.

Serves 4 to 6.

TUNISIA
Anise, Fennel or Dill Root Salad

IN TUNISIA, THE WEATHER IS DRY AND HOT. Ice water is served flavored with anise, fennel or dill. The green part of the plant is cut off and placed in a pitcher of water, which is then refrigerated. What to do with the root? Slice it into very thin slices, dress it with lemon juice and olive oil and serve it as a *mezze* salad.

1½-2 cups very thinly sliced anise root, fennel root or dill root	½ teaspoon salt
3 tablespoons lemon juice	Pepper or *harissa*
2 tablespoons extra-virgin olive oil	(hot pepper sauce) to taste

Place the sliced root in a glass or ceramic bowl. In a small bowl, whisk together the lemon juice, olive oil, salt and pepper or *harissa*. Pour the mixture over the root, toss, then refrigerate for several hours, allowing the salad to marinate. Serve at room temperature.

Serves 4 to 6.

LEBANON/SYRIA

Tabbouleh

(Bulgur Salad)

MY CHILDREN LOVE PARSLEY SO MUCH that they fight over who gets to eat more. When they were little, Yacov used to tell them that if they ate green vegetables their eyes would become green. This traditional tabbouleh is much greener than American versions.

½ cup fine bulgur	3 large tomatoes, finely chopped
1 teaspoon salt	8-10 green onions, finely chopped
¼ teaspoon pepper	¼ cup finely chopped fresh mint
¼ teaspoon cinnamon	¼ cup lemon juice
¼ teaspoon allspice	¼ cup olive oil
¼ teaspoon nutmeg	Romaine lettuce leaves
5 cups finely chopped fresh parsley leaves	for serving

Wash the bulgur and drain well by squeezing out the excess water with cupped hands. Place in a bowl and refrigerate for at least 1 hour.

Add the salt, pepper and spices to the bulgur and mix. Add the parsley, tomatoes, green onions and mint. The mixture can be refrigerated for several hours more.

Just before serving, whisk together the lemon juice and olive oil. Pour the dressing over the salad and toss well. Serve at room temperature. Use the romaine lettuce leaves to scoop up the salad.

Serves 6.

Lebanon/Syria
Falafel

THESE CHICKPEA FRITTERS ARE SERVED AS A SIDE DISH with Tahina (page 38) and an assortment of salads, or in pita bread as a snack or light meal.

2 15-ounce cans chickpeas (garbanzo beans), or about 2½ cups cooked	2 garlic cloves, minced
	1½ teaspoons cumin
2 slices good-quality white bread	1½ teaspoons salt (if using freshly cooked beans; canned beans need no salt)
2 tablespoons all-purpose flour	
½ teaspoon baking soda	
½ cup chopped onion	Vegetable oil for frying
½ cup finely chopped fresh parsley	

Drain the chickpeas and place them in a food processor fitted with the metal blade. Add the bread and process. Add the remaining ingredients and blend well. Let stand for 15 minutes. Roll the mixture into small balls about 1½ inches in diameter or into patties about 2 inches across.

In a large deep pot, heat 2 to 3 inches of oil to 350°F; a cube of bread tossed in will brown quickly. Drop several balls or patties into the hot oil and cook, turning to brown on all sides. Remove with a slotted spoon and set aside on paper towels to drain. Serve immediately or keep warm in the oven, wrapped in foil.

Makes about 20 falafel balls or patties.

LEBANON/SYRIA
Tahina

IT'S HARD TO GO WRONG with this delicious creamy-white dip made with sesame seed paste, garlic and lemon juice. I sometimes add more water to make a dressing for falafel, vegetables and salads. It can be made by hand or in a food processor or blender.

2 garlic cloves

½ teaspoon salt, or to taste

1 cup tahini (sesame seed paste)

½ cup lemon juice, or to taste

About ¼ cup water

In a mortar or small bowl, crush the garlic with the salt. Transfer the garlic paste to a larger bowl and blend in the tahini with a fork, spoon or whisk. Whisk in the lemon juice. Add enough water to make the sauce the consistency of mayonnaise.

Serve in a bowl or on a plate with pita bread.

Makes 1¾ to 2 cups.

LEBANON/SYRIA
Hummus

THIS LEBANESE VERSION OF HUMMUS, a tan-colored puree of chickpeas and tahini, is garnished with toasted pine nuts; it can also be topped with more chickpeas. Serve with pita bread.

2 cups cooked chickpeas (garbanzo beans), drained

3 garlic cloves, crushed

1 cup tahini (sesame seed paste)
Juice from 2 lemons, or to taste

½ teaspoon salt, or to taste

¼ cup pine nuts or handful of cooked chickpeas for garnish
Olive oil for garnish
Paprika or cayenne pepper for garnish

In a food processor fitted with the metal blade, puree the chickpeas and garlic. Add the tahini, lemon juice and salt. Continue to blend until smooth and creamy. Add a little water for a smoother consistency, if desired.

If you are using the pine nuts for garnish, toast them in a small skillet over medium-high heat, stirring occasionally, for about 4 minutes, or until golden. Set aside to cool.

To serve, spoon the hummus onto a serving plate or into a serving bowl. Make a slight hollow in the center of the mound and place the pine nuts or whole chickpeas in it. Drizzle a little olive oil on top and sprinkle with paprika or cayenne. Serve chilled or at room temperature.

Makes 3 cups; serves 6.

LEBANON/SYRIA
Eggplant and Tahini Dip
(Baba Ghanoush)

BABA GHANOUSH, another Middle Eastern *mezze* favorite, is a rather bland-looking dip with amazing flavors. The taste of charred eggplant skin resonates through it. The eggplants are traditionally roasted over open fires, but I use my broiler for a similar effect.

2	large eggplants, pierced several times on each side with a fork	2	garlic cloves
¼	cup tahini (sesame seed paste)	1	teaspoon salt
¼	cup lemon juice	¼	cup finely chopped fresh parsley for garnish

Preheat the broiler, with a rack about 5 inches from the heat. Place the eggplants under the broiler and broil, turning, until the outer skin is charred and becomes loose, about 15 minutes. Remove the eggplants from the heat and let them cool in a colander in the kitchen sink, then peel off the skin and scoop out the pulp into a medium bowl. Discard the skin. Mash the pulp with the tahini and lemon juice. In a mortar or small bowl, crush the garlic with the salt and add it to the eggplant mixture. Adjust the seasoning, adding more salt or lemon juice if desired. Transfer the dip to a shallow bowl or plate, garnish with a sprinkle of parsley and serve at room temperature.

Makes 2 cups; serves 6.

INDIA
Indian Vegetable Fritters
(Pakoras)

THESE BOMBAY FRITTERS are vegetables dipped in a chickpea batter and fried into a golden appetizer. Serve them with samosas and chutneys.

Batter

1	cup chickpea flour
1	teaspoon salt
¼	teaspoon baking powder
1	tablespoon cumin
1	tablespoon black mustard seeds
½	teaspoon coriander
½	teaspoon turmeric
	Pinch of cayenne (optional)

¾	cup water
1	teaspoon vegetable oil, plus several cups for frying
3-4	cups vegetables: use a variety, such as cauliflower florets, broccoli florets, bell peppers seeded and cut into strips, mushrooms and carrots, parsnips or potatoes, cut into ½-inch slices

To make the batter: Combine the chickpea flour, salt, baking powder and spices in a large bowl. Stir in the water and 1 teaspoon oil; the consistency should be like pancake batter. Add a little more water if necessary. Let stand for at least 15 minutes before using.

Pour about 3 inches of vegetable oil into a large deep pot and heat to 350°F; a cube of bread tossed in will brown quickly. Dip the vegetable pieces into the batter, making sure that they are coated on all sides. Drop them one at a time into the hot oil. Fry, turning, until they are golden brown. Remove with a slotted spoon and drain on paper towels. Serve with Fresh Cilantro-Mint Chutney (page 256).

Serves 6.

GREECE

Stuffed Grape Leaves
(Dolmas)

MY AFFINITY FOR GREEK CUISINE began as a child when a friend of mine shared some stuffed grape leaves and spinach-and-cheese filo snacks she had brought to school for lunch. Over the years, I have tried many stuffed grape leaf recipes; every Mediterranean country has a slightly different version. This is the recipe that I prefer, which combines the flavors of currants and pine nuts. Stuffed grape leaves can also be made with ground meat and rice, although I favor the vegetarian version.

When I prepare stuffed grape leaves, I triple the recipe and freeze about 50 of the rolled grape leaves for cooking at a later time. To do this, place the rolled leaves that are to be frozen on a plate, leaving a generous space between them. Freeze them uncovered for 1 hour, then remove them from the plate and package them neatly in storage bags or airtight containers. To serve, thaw at room temperature and continue cooking as directed.

¼   cup pine nuts

2   tablespoons olive oil

1   cup minced onion

2   garlic cloves, minced

¼   cup dried currants

1   cup long-grain white rice, soaked in cold water and drained

½   teaspoon allspice

1   teaspoon salt, or to taste

½   teaspoon pepper, or to taste

3   tablespoons minced fresh parsley

2   tablespoons minced fresh mint

1   large jar grape leaves, or about 35 fresh small leaves, plus 5-10 more for lining the pot

¼   cup lemon juice (from 2 lemons)

1   cup chicken broth or water

In a medium skillet, sauté the pine nuts over medium heat in 1 tablespoon of the oil. When they have turned golden, remove with a slotted spoon and set aside. Add the onion, garlic and currants to the skillet and sauté for 2 to 3 minutes. Add the rice, allspice, salt and pepper and sauté until the rice becomes translucent, about 3 minutes.

Remove from the heat and transfer into a medium bowl. Stir in the pine nuts, parsley and mint. Let cool.

If using fresh grape leaves, dip 35 leaves in boiling water for 1 minute. Drain. Cut off the stems and pat each leaf dry.

Place 1 heaping tablespoon of the filling in the center of each grape leaf. Fold the end of the leaf over to cover the filling. Fold in the sides, and starting from the stem end, roll the leaf up gently to form a cylinder.

Place a flat layer of grape leaves in a heavy saucepan to insulate the stuffed leaves from the heat while they cook. You can substitute lemon slices or tomato slices; both will provide flavor. Place the stuffed grape leaves side by side in the saucepan. I prefer to cook them in a single layer, but if this is not possible, layer them until all are used.

In a small bowl, combine the lemon juice with the broth or water and the remaining 1 tablespoon olive oil. Pour the mixture over the stuffed grape leaves. Place a heavy plate on top of the grape leaves to weight them. Bring to a boil, then reduce heat to low, cover and simmer for 30 minutes, or until all liquids have been absorbed.

Makes 35 stuffed grape leaves.

SYRIA
Fried Bulgur Dumplings with Meat Filling
(Kibbe)

KIBBE IS THE NATIONAL DISH of both Syria and Lebanon. The basic concept is a combination of fine bulgur and ground meat. The meat must be very fresh and very lean and is ground twice. In the past, women spent hours grinding it with a mortar and pestle, but modern appliances have taken the effort and production out of grinding. The mixture of bulgur and meat is shaped into ovals, stuffed with a filling of meat and pine nuts and fried, then served with hummus, tahina, baba ghanoush and tabbouleh. I also like the *kibbe* as a main dish with salad and tahina. Make the full amount and freeze the extras. The recipe was given to me by Hugette Galante, a wonderful cook.

Dough	Meat filling
2½ cups (a 16-ounce bag) fine bulgur	2 tablespoons olive oil
1 cup matzo meal	½ cup pine nuts
½ pound fresh, lean ground beef, lamb or turkey, twice ground	1 medium onion, chopped
	1½ pounds ground beef, lamb or turkey
1 cup all-purpose flour	1 teaspoon allspice
2 tablespoons olive oil	1 teaspoon cinnamon (cumin can be substituted)
1 tablespoon salt	1 teaspoon salt
1 tablespoon cumin	
1 tablespoon water (optional)	Vegetable oil for frying

To make the dough: Wash the bulgur, cover with water and soak it for 15 minutes, or until the water is absorbed. Squeeze out the excess water. Add the matzo meal, ground meat, flour, oil and spices, kneading the dough by hand; the texture should be firm but pliable. Add water, if necessary, for more moisture. Cover and set aside.

To make the filling: In a large skillet, heat the oil over medium-high heat and sauté the pine nuts until golden. Remove with a slotted spoon and set aside. Add the onion to the skillet and sauté until softened, about 5 minutes. Add the meat and cook, breaking it up with a wooden spoon, until the liquid has evaporated. Remove from the heat, and when it is cool, add the seasonings.

To make the dumplings: Shape the dough into ovals the size of a large egg. Push your forefinger into the center of the oval. Continue to shape the oval into a hollow cylinder about the length of a finger. Fill with meat filling. Close the top by pinching to form a point. (Any extra filling can be frozen for future use. If you are preparing the *kibbe* for another time, you can place them in storage bags and freeze them on a plate. When you are ready to use them, do not thaw; fry them frozen.)

Preheat the oven to 200°F.

Pour about 3 inches of oil into a deep pan and heat to 350°F; a cube of bread tossed into the pan will brown quickly. Immerse a couple of *kibbe* at a time, frying them until they are golden brown, about 3 minutes. Remove them with a slotted spoon, placing them on paper towels to drain. Place them in a baking dish in the warm oven while you fry the remainder. Serve hot or cold.

Makes 36 kibbe balls.

RHODES
Cheese-Filled Pastries
(Boyo de Queso)

THESE LITTLE STUFFED CYLINDRICAL PACKAGES make wonderful appetizers because they are compact and easy to serve and can be made well ahead of time. Because feta cheese is very salty, it should be mixed with a blander cheese for balance. The addition of mashed potatoes makes a light, fluffy filling.

This recipe will yield about 80 pastries. Do not be deceived by the quantity: my family of five can finish nearly half a batch before I am ready to serve them. If you do freeze a batch, let the pastries thaw for 30 minutes before baking.

Filling
1 pound hoop cheese or another
   semisoft white cheese such as
   ricotta or pot cheese
1 pound feta cheese
1 cup mashed potatoes
2 large eggs

1 16-ounce package filo dough
   (found in the frozen-food
   section of most supermarkets)
8 tablespoons (1 stick) margarine
   or butter, melted

To make the filling: Blend all the filling ingredients together in a food processor fitted with the metal blade or by hand in a large bowl to make a smooth paste.

Preheat the oven to 350°F and lightly grease 2 cookie sheets.

The trick to this recipe is in the handling of the filo dough. Cut the stack of filo leaves in half lengthwise and then in half again (figure 1). Work with 1 stack at a time, forming each pastry on top of the stack. Cover the stacks you are not using with a damp clean dish towel so that they do not become dry or brittle.

With a pastry brush, lightly brush the top of 1 piece of filo with melted margarine or butter, then turn it over so that it adheres to the piece below it. Place 1 teaspoon of filling in the center, 1 inch from the top of one end of the sheet, and spread it across to form a horizontal line (figure 2). Do not overstuff the pastries or they will burst. Carefully roll up the

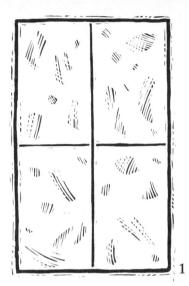

pastry sheet from the filling end to make a small cigar-shaped pastry (figure 3). Repeat until all pastry sheets are used and there is no more filling.

Transfer the pastries to the cookie sheets and bake until golden, about 20 minutes.

Makes 80 pastries.

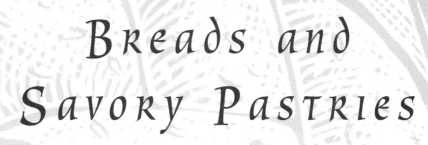

Breads and Savory Pastries

Recipes

Syria/Lebanon
Pita Bread

THE EASIEST WAY TO PREPARE THE DOUGH FOR PITA BREAD is to put all the ingredients into a bread machine and let the machine do the work.

2 packages (4½ teaspoons) active dry yeast	4 cups all-purpose flour
1 teaspoon sugar	1 teaspoon salt
1¼ cups warm water	1 teaspoon olive oil

Combine the yeast and sugar in a small bowl. Add the warm water and stir until the dry ingredients have dissolved. Put the flour and salt in a large bowl, add the yeast mixture and stir with a wooden spoon until a smooth, firm dough is formed. Turn out the dough onto a lightly floured surface and knead for 8 to 10 minutes, or until smooth and elastic.

Place the dough ball in a large bowl greased with the oil. Cover with a clean dish towel and let rest for 1 hour, or until the dough has doubled in bulk. Divide the dough into 12 golfball-sized balls. Roll out each ball until it is ⅛ inch thick and about 5 inches in diameter. Cover the rolled-out circles with a clean dish towel and let rise in a warm place for 30 minutes.

About 15 minutes before baking, preheat the oven to 475°F. Grease a baking sheet.

Roll out each circle again. Transfer the dough circles to 2 baking sheets and spray a light mist of water over them. Bake the pitas for 3 minutes, or until they have puffed up and are lightly golden. Cool on a rack for about 1 hour. The pitas may be stored in plastic bags and kept at room temperature for up to 3 days or frozen for up to 3 months. (Do not wrap the bread while it is still warm.)

Makes 12 pitas.

Yemenite White Bread

(Jahnun)

EMENITE BREADS HAVE BECOME VERY POPULAR IN ISRAEL because of their delicate, pastrylike layers and rich flavor. Both qualities are the result of patience, love and a lot of kneading. Although traditionally done completely by hand, the labor of making this sweet white bread is effectively shortened with the use of a modern food processor. Traditionally, the bread is made with lots of butter and baked overnight in a low oven so that it can be served fresh on Shabbat morning without kindling a flame. The following recipe has been revised so that it bakes in 30 minutes and uses less butter than traditional versions. If you are serving it with poultry or meat, make it with nondairy margarine. This loaf pulls apart easily into six sections.

3¾	cups all-purpose flour	1	cup water
½	cup sugar	1	large egg
1½	teaspoons salt	8	tablespoons (1 stick) margarine
1	teaspoon baking soda		or butter, softened

Combine all the dry ingredients in a food processor fitted with the metal blade, pulsing to blend the ingredients. In a small bowl, lightly beat the egg and water. Slowly add the mixture to the food processor in a thin stream while the motor is running, processing until the dough becomes smooth and stiff. It will be a little sticky but should not be watery. Alternatively, if you are mixing by hand, combine the dry ingredients in a large bowl and stir the water and egg mixture in with a wooden spoon, then turn out the dough onto a lightly floured surface and knead until it is smooth.

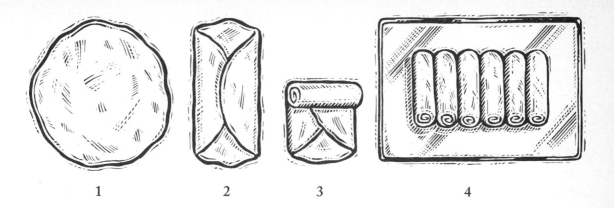

1   2   3   4

Remove the dough from the food processor or the bowl and let stand for 15 minutes in a clean bowl, covered with a clean dish towel. Knead for 5 minutes; set aside for another 15 minutes.

Divide the dough into 6 equal portions and roll into balls the size of small limes. Transfer the dough balls to an oiled plate, cover with plastic wrap and let rest for at least 2 hours so that the dough will relax.

Preheat the oven to 350°F or to 200°F if baking overnight.

Flatten each ball on a work surface such as a bread board that has been coated with margarine or butter. Roll and stretch each ball into a circle until it is so thin that you can almost see through it (figure 1). Using a pastry brush or your hand, gently spread a layer of margarine or butter across the surface of the dough.

Working with 1 circle of dough at a time, fold 1 outer side inward, then the opposite side (figure 2). Coat with margarine or butter, then slowly roll it up into a cylinder (figure 3). Place the cylinders side by side, ½ inch apart, on a shallow baking sheet (figure 4). Let stand for 15 minutes, then bake for 30 minutes at 350°F (or overnight at 200°F), until the top is golden. Serve warm, pulled apart into 6 sections.

Makes 1 loaf; divides into 6 sections.

White Rolls
(Kubana)

KUBANA IS MADE OF A SWEET BREAD DOUGH similar to challah dough. Small portions of dough are placed side by side in the pan, where they rise and press together while baking. This recipe calls for less butter than traditional ones, and the bread is baked in a cake pan.

2	teaspoons active dry yeast	1	teaspoon salt
1	teaspoon plus 6 tablespoons sugar	2	tablespoons margarine or butter,
1½	cups lukewarm water		cut into pieces, plus 4 tablespoons
3½	cups all-purpose flour		

Combine the yeast with 1 teaspoon of the sugar and ¼ cup of the lukewarm water in a small bowl.

In a food processor fitted with the metal blade, blend the flour and salt. Combine the remaining 6 tablespoons sugar and the 2 tablespoons margarine or butter with the yeast mixture. With the motor running, slowly pour the yeast mixture into the flour in the processor, then with the motor still running, pour 1 cup of the warm water into the processor in a thin stream. Add the remaining ¼ cup water a tablespoon at a time. Process until the dough is smooth and firm. Alternatively, you can mix the dough by hand by combining the flour and salt in a large bowl and stirring in the yeast mixture with a wooden spoon.

Turn out the dough onto a lightly floured surface and knead until smooth and firm, 10 to 15 minutes. Transfer the dough to a large clean bowl, cover with a clean dish towel and set aside for 1 hour, or until doubled in volume.

Turn the dough out onto a work surface and knead for 5 minutes. Set aside to rest for 30 minutes, uncovered.

Divide the dough into 8 pieces the size of small lemons. In a shallow pot, melt the remaining margarine or butter and dip each ball into it. Arrange the balls in a cake pan, placing 1 in the center and 7 balls in a circle around it. Cover the pan with a clean dish towel. Set aside for 2 hours, or until the dough doubles in bulk.

Preheat the oven to 350°F (or to 200°F, if you plan to bake the bread overnight). Bake for about 25 minutes, or until the bread is golden on top. Cool on a rack.

Makes 1 loaf; divides into 8 rolls.

YEMEN

Yemenite Flatbread
(Melawach)

MY SON, JONATHAN, IS A FINICKY EATER, but he loves this bread and always suggests that I make more. Unfortunately, *melawach* is not a spur-of-the-moment thing. The dough is stretched, buttered and rolled, then refrigerated, creating a fine, multilayered bread. It is then cooked in a skillet on top of the stove. Luckily, you can make it ahead when you're in the mood and freeze it.

3¼	cups all-purpose flour	1	large egg
2	tablespoons sugar	4-8	tablespoons (½-1 stick) margarine
1½	teaspoons salt		or butter, softened, plus a little
1	teaspoon baking soda		more for greasing the work
1	cup water		surface

Combine all the dry ingredients in a food processor fitted with the metal blade, pulsing to blend the ingredients. With the motor running, slowly add the water and egg in a thin stream. Continue to process for about 5 minutes, until the dough becomes smooth and stiff.

Transfer to a clean bowl and let the dough rest, uncovered, for 15 minutes so that it relaxes. Knead again for 5 minutes, then set aside for another 15 minutes.

Divide the dough into 6 portions and roll into balls (figure 1). Place the dough balls on an oiled plate, cover with plastic wrap and refrigerate for at least 3 hours.

Flatten each ball on a work surface coated with margarine or butter (figure 2). Roll and stretch each ball so thin that you can almost see through it; the dough should be elastic and pliable (figure 3). Using a pastry brush or your hand, gently spread a layer of margarine or but-

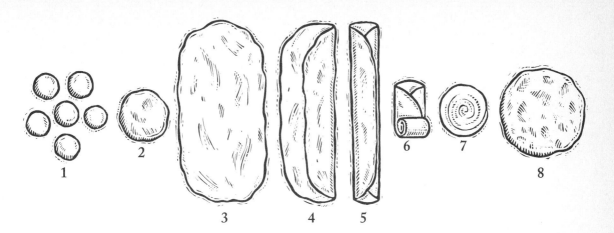

ter across the surface of the dough. Fold the dough into thirds by folding 1 side about 4 inches in and then the opposite side 4 inches in, as though you are folding a letter (figures 4 and 5). Roll out again, coat with margarine or butter and refold as before. Coat with margarine or butter and slowly roll up each piece of dough like a jelly roll (figure 6), then flatten (figure 7). (At this point the dough rolls can be wrapped in plastic wrap and frozen for future use or refrigerated for up to 3 hours. If frozen, thaw overnight when ready to use.)

When you are ready to cook the bread, choose a large skillet. Further flatten each ball with your hands until it is as large as the interior of the skillet (figure 8). Heat the skillet and add the pancake to the dry skillet. Fry each pancake, one at a time, over high heat for several minutes until browned, then flip and fry the other side. Reduce the heat and cook the flatbread for several minutes more. Serve hot.

Makes 6 large flatbreads.

Indian Flatbread
(Naan)

TRADITIONALLY, THESE BREADS ARE BAKED in hot clay ovens, but making them in an ordinary oven on a cookie sheet, baking stone or inverted baking sheet gives fine results. Serve them plain or with one of the optional toppings suggested in the recipe.

2 cups bread flour	1 tablespoon margarine
1¼ teaspoons active dry yeast	or butter, melted
1 teaspoon sugar	Sesame seeds, poppy seeds,
½ teaspoon salt	minced garlic or chopped chives
3 tablespoons vegetable oil	for topping (optional)
About ¾ cup water	

Combine the flour, yeast, sugar and salt in a food processor fitted with the plastic blade, in a bread machine or in a large mixing bowl. If using a food processor, combine by pulsing. Add 2 tablespoons of the oil and slowly add enough of the water to create a smooth, elastic dough ball.

Put the remaining 1 tablespoon oil in a large bowl. Place the dough ball in the bowl, turning it several times to coat all sides with the oil. Cover the bowl with a clean dish towel and set aside to rise at room temperature for 1½ hours.

Preheat the oven to 475°F.

Remove the dough from the bowl, punch down and knead for 2 minutes. Divide the dough into 4 balls. Allow the balls to rest for 10 minutes, then roll out into long ovals ¼ inch thick. Place the ovals on baking sheets and brush with the melted margarine or butter. Sprinkle with the toppings, if using. Bake for about 8 minutes, or until the bread puffs up a little and turns lightly golden. Serve warm.

Makes 4 flatbreads.

Tunisian Fried Sandwiches
(Les Fricassées)

LES FRICASSÉES ARE SMALL BREAD MOUNDS that are fried and stuffed with a variety of fillings and eaten like sandwiches. My friend Serge Cohen sometimes makes them the size of rolls and serves them as an appetizer.

Dough

1 cube fresh yeast, or 1 package
  (2¼ teaspoons) active dry yeast
¾ cup lukewarm water
2¼ cups all-purpose flour
1 teaspoon salt
1 large egg
3 tablespoons vegetable oil

Filling

1 6-ounce can solid white tuna,
  drained and broken into chunks
2 medium new potatoes,
  boiled and sliced
2 large tomatoes, sliced
3 hard-boiled eggs, peeled and sliced
1 medium cucumber, peeled
  and sliced
2 tablespoons chopped fresh cilantro
2 tablespoons capers, drained
  Handful of green and/or
    black olives
  Salt and pepper to taste

Vegetable oil for frying

Harissa (hot pepper sauce), optional

To make the dough: Mix the yeast in a liquid measuring cup with the water and let stand for 15 minutes, until foamy.

In a food processor fitted with the metal blade, combine the flour and salt, then add the egg, oil and yeast mixture. Process until the dough is smooth, about 5 minutes. Knead the dough on a floured bread board for 5 minutes. Divide it into 8 golfball-sized balls. Roll each ball into an oval and set on a clean dish towel to rise, covered with another dish towel, for 1 hour in a warm corner of your kitchen (usually close to your oven).

To make the filling: On a large platter, arrange the tuna, potatoes, tomatoes, eggs and cucumber. Sprinkle with the cilantro, capers, olives and salt and pepper.

Pour 3 inches of oil into a deep pot or wok-type fryer and heat the oil to 350°F; a cube of bread tossed in will brown quickly. Fry several balls at a time, turning until they become golden brown, about 5 minutes. Remove with a slotted spoon and drain on paper towels.

Make a slit across the long side of the fried bread, open each one and stuff with the filling ingredients, adding a little *harissa*, if desired. Serve immediately.

Makes 8 fried sandwiches.

IRAQ

Turnovers Stuffed with Ground Meat and Pine Nuts

(Sembussak)

YOU CAN MAKE A VEGETARIAN VERSION of these fried turnovers by substituting ground chickpeas for the meat and replacing the allspice and cinnamon with cumin. Both versions are very popular as a snack or as part of the *mezze*. Ground turkey or lamb can be used in place of the beef.

Meat Filling

1	tablespoon olive oil
¼	cup pine nuts
1	medium onion, finely chopped
1	pound ground beef, turkey or lamb
¼	teaspoon allspice
¼	teaspoon cinnamon
½	teaspoon salt, or to taste

Dough

3	cups all-purpose flour
1	teaspoon active dry yeast
½	teaspoon salt
½	teaspoon sugar
1	cup lukewarm water

Vegetable oil for frying

To make the meat filling: Heat the oil in a large skillet, add the pine nuts and sauté for about 1 minute, or until lightly golden. Remove with a slotted spoon and set aside. Add the onion to the skillet and sauté over medium-high heat until transparent, 2 to 3 minutes. Add the meat and cook, stirring to break up any clumps with a wooden spoon, until browned. Cool and stir in the seasonings and pine nuts.

To make the dough: Place the flour in a food processor fitted with the metal blade.

Combine the yeast, salt, sugar and water in a measuring cup or any other cup with a spout. Pour the yeast mixture into the flour, pulsing to combine. Process until a smooth dough ball is formed. Let the dough rest for 15 minutes, then turn it out onto a floured bread board. Roll the dough out to ⅛ inch thick. Cut out 18 to 20 circles using the rim of a drinking glass.

Place 1 teaspoon of the filling in the center of each circle and fold the dough over to form a half-moon. Pinch the edges firmly.

Pour about 3 inches of oil into a deep pot and heat to 350°F; a cube of bread tossed in will brown quickly. Place the stuffed pastries into the oil in batches; do not crowd. Cook until golden brown, then turn and cook the other side until golden, 3 to 5 minutes. Remove with a slotted spoon and drain on paper towels.

Makes 18 to 20 turnovers.

VARIATION

Chickpea Filling

This recipe can also be used in any meat-filled pastry that you wish to make vegetarian.

1 tablespoon olive oil	1 teaspoon cumin
1 large onion, finely chopped	½ teaspoon salt
1 14-ounce can chickpeas (garbanzo beans), drained	Pepper to taste

Heat the oil in a large skillet, add the onion and sauté for 3 to 5 minutes, or until translucent. Add the chickpeas, cumin, salt and pepper and continue to sauté for 3 to 5 minutes more, or until heated through. Transfer the mixture to a bowl and mash with a fork until a paste is formed. The mixture should be the consistency of mashed potatoes.

Savory Turnovers
(Borekas)

OREKAS ARE TO THE MIDDLE EAST what croissants are to France. Every bakery and many roadside stands sell them in various sizes, brimming with potato, spinach, eggplant or cheese fillings. *Borekas* that are sold commercially have a fine, flaky pastry, almost like puff pastry dough, which can be bought and substituted. However, the cooks I know make their own dough, which is denser and less flaky. *Borekas* are usually eaten for snacks, dairy brunches or as part of a Shabbat morning meal.

Dough

- 3 cups all-purpose flour
- 8 tablespoons (1 stick) margarine or butter, cut into pieces
- ½ teaspoon salt (if using unsalted margarine or butter)
- 1 cup water

Eggplant Filling

- 1 large eggplant
- ½ cup crumbled feta cheese
- ½ cup grated Gruyère cheese

Potato and Cheese Filling

- 1 boiling potato, peeled, boiled and mashed
- 1 large egg, beaten
- 1 cup crumbled feta cheese

- 1 egg yolk, mixed with 1 teaspoon water, for brushing on turnovers
  Sesame seeds or grated cheese for sprinkling on turnovers

To make the dough: Preheat the oven to 400°F. Lightly oil 2 baking sheets. Put the flour, margarine or butter and salt, if using, in a food processor fitted with the metal blade. Add the water and process, pulsing to combine, until the dough forms a ball. Alternatively, put the flour (and salt, if using) in a large bowl and cut in the margarine or butter, using 2 knives or a pastry cutter, and stir in the water. Turn the dough out and knead until it is smooth, about 8 minutes. Divide the dough into 18 to 20 balls the size of large walnuts. Let stand for 15 minutes before rolling them out.

To make the eggplant filling: If you are planning to broil the eggplant, place it on a baking sheet and preheat the broiler, with a rack about 5 inches from the heat. Broil the eggplant until tender, about 15 to 20 minutes, or until the outer skin becomes charred. (Alternatively, to roast the eggplant over a flame, attach the eggplant to a long-pronged fork with a wooden handle. Hold the eggplant over an open gas flame, 1 to 2 inches above the flame, turning it to roast on all sides. The skin should be dark and slightly brittle but not black.)

Remove and discard the peel. Squeeze the eggplant to remove excess liquid. In a food processor fitted with the metal blade, blend the eggplant with the cheeses or mash together with a fork.

To make the potato and cheese filling: In a food processor or by hand, blend the ingredients until smooth.

To form the turnovers: Roll each ball out flat on a lightly floured surface. Place a teaspoon of the filling into the center of the circle and fold over to form a semicircle. Seal each pastry by pressing along the edges with your thumb or the end of a fork. Brush the top with the beaten egg, then dip into sesame seeds or sprinkle with grated cheese. Place on baking sheets.

Bake for 20 minutes, or until the tops are golden. Serve warm or at room temperature.

Makes 18 to 20 turnovers.

TURKEY
Savory Stuffed Yeast Pastries
(Bolemas)

THESE BOLEMAS ARE MUCH EASIER to make than they look. The recipe was a gift from Rebecca Levy, who has spent her life serving the Sephardic community in Los Angeles. Originally from Rhodes, she is a perfectionist when it comes to pastries.

Starter

1	teaspoon active dry yeast
½	teaspoon sugar
	Pinch of salt
1	cup lukewarm water
1	tablespoon all-purpose flour

Dough

3	cups all-purpose flour
1	teaspoon salt
1	teaspoon margarine or butter, melted
½	cup vegetable oil

Spinach Filling

1	10-ounce bag spinach, washed, patted dry, stemmed and finely chopped
½	pound kashkaval or feta cheese, crumbled
1-2	tablespoons bread crumbs
¼	teaspoon dried dill (optional)
1	large egg
	Pinch of salt and white pepper

Pumpkin Filling

2	cups canned pumpkin
1	large egg, beaten
1	cup crumbled kashkaval or feta cheese
½	cup grated Parmesan cheese
½	teaspoon salt
½	teaspoon cinnamon
2	tablespoons grated Kefalotiri or Parmesan cheese for topping

To make the starter: Dissolve the yeast, sugar and salt in the lukewarm water in a small bowl. Stir in the flour and set aside for 10 minutes, or until bubbly.

To make the dough: In a large mixing bowl, combine the flour, salt and margarine or butter. Slowly add the starter, stirring to form a soft dough. Knead the dough well and divide it into about 18 pieces that are a little smaller than golfballs. Put the balls in a shallow pan and pour the oil over them. Turn the balls to make sure all sides are coated. Let rise for 30 minutes. Meanwhile, make one of the fillings.

To make the spinach filling: Mix all the ingredients together well in a large bowl or use a food processor fitted with the metal blade, pulsing just enough to blend.

To make the pumpkin filling: Mix all the ingredients together well in a large bowl or in a food processor.

Preheat the oven to 350°F. Lightly oil 2 baking sheets.

To form the pastries: Remove 1 ball at a time from the bowl. Pat and stretch it as far as possible without making holes. Next, shape the stretched pastry dough into a rectangle measuring about 5½ x 10 inches. Spread a stripe of filling along the long side of 1 edge (figure 1). Then roll the dough up like a jelly roll (figure 2). Turn the roll into a coil shape (figure 3). Sprinkle the top with grated cheese (figure 4).

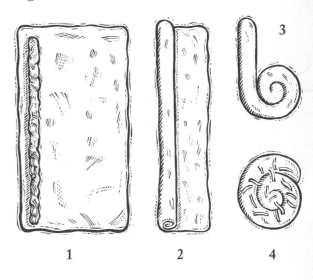

Set the coils on the baking sheets. Bake for 25 minutes, or until the tops are lightly golden.

Makes about 18 pastries.

TUNISIA
Fried Pastries with Potato Filling
(Brik)

BRIK IS TO TUNISIA WHAT FALAFEL IS TO ISRAEL: the national snack food. A light, fried savory pastry, it is sold at roadside stands and on the beach, in many forms and with various fillings.

Because the traditional dough for *brik* is very difficult to make at home, egg roll skins are sometimes used as a substitute, much to the dissatisfaction of those in the know. Another pastry-dough product, called *lumpia* (sold in Korean, Philippine and Asian markets), is closer to the traditional dough wrapping. The following recipe uses a pareve filling, which means that it can be served before a dairy or meat meal.

12 sheets spring roll skins (the thinnest egg roll skins) or *lumpia*	½ cup finely chopped fresh parsley
	1 large egg
	½ pound (2 medium) boiling potatoes, peeled, boiled and mashed
2 tablespoons vegetable oil, plus more for frying	1 egg white, lightly beaten
1 medium onion, finely chopped	
4 garlic cloves, minced	

In a medium skillet, heat the 2 tablespoons oil, add the onion and garlic and sauté until browned, about 3 minutes. Stir in the parsley and sauté for 1 minute more. Remove from the heat, cool, mix in the egg and mashed potatoes and set aside.

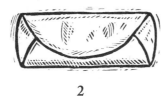

1

2

3

4

Working with 1 spring roll or *lumpia* sheet at a time, place a tablespoon of filling in the center (figure 1). Fold the top and bottom edges over the filling as though you are folding a business letter (figure 2). Fold in the sides to form a rectangle or square (figures 3 and 4). Brush the edges of the turnovers with egg white to keep them closed.

Pour oil into a large skillet to a depth of 1 inch. Heat to 350°F; a cube of bread tossed in will brown quickly. Place the turnovers in the hot oil one at a time. Fry until golden, turning once, about 1½ minutes per side. Remove with a slotted spoon and drain on paper towels. Serve immediately.

Makes 12 turnovers.

India

Deep-Fried Vegetable Pastries

(Samosas)

HE OLDEST JEWISH COMMUNITY IN INDIA was the Bene Israel of Bombay. According to legend, it started out as a group of shipwrecked Jews: seven men and seven women who were washed ashore around 175 B.C.E. Their cuisine was basically Indian, and they observed Kashrut.

The woman who gave me this recipe came from the community in Bombay. These vegetable-filled pastries can be served as an appetizer or side dish.

Dough

3 cups all-purpose flour

1 teaspoon salt

¼ cup vegetable oil, plus
1 tablespoon for oiling the bowl

¾ cup water

Potato Filling

2 tablespoons vegetable oil

½ teaspoon black mustard seeds

½ cup finely chopped onion

2 teaspoons peeled and finely chopped fresh ginger

1 teaspoon fennel seeds

¼ teaspoon cumin

¼ teaspoon turmeric

2 boiling potatoes, peeled, boiled and cubed

½ cup fresh or frozen peas

½ teaspoon salt

1 tablespoon water

1 tablespoon finely chopped fresh cilantro

½ teaspoon garam masala (Indian spice combination found in Indian markets and other specialty shops)

3 cups vegetable oil for frying

To make the dough: In a large bowl, combine the flour, salt and ¼ cup oil, working the dough with your fingers to create a coarse meal. Pour in the water and knead vigorously for about 5 minutes, until a ball forms. Add extra water if needed, a tablespoon at a time. Turn the dough out of the bowl and continue kneading until smooth. Wash out the mixing bowl and place 1 tablespoon oil in the bottom. Roll the ball in the oil several times so that all sides are coated. Cover the bowl with a damp clean dish towel and let the dough rest for 2 hours at room temperature.

Meanwhile, make the filling: In a medium skillet, heat the oil. When it is hot, add the mustard seeds; when they crackle and begin to burst, add the onion and ginger. Sauté until the onion is soft, about 3 minutes. Add the fennel, cumin and turmeric, stirring. Add the potatoes, peas, salt and water.

Reduce the heat, cover and cook for 5 minutes to combine the flavors. Stir in the cilantro and the garam masala. Remove from the heat and set aside.

To prepare the samosas: Pinch off a piece of dough the size of a large walnut, keeping the rest of the dough covered. On a lightly floured surface, roll the ball into a flat disk about 4 inches in diameter. Place 1 teaspoon of filling in the center of the circle and fold over to create a semicircle. Moisten the inner edges with water and pinch them closed. Lay each samosa flat on a plate and cover with plastic wrap or foil until all of them are ready for deep-frying.

To deep-fry, heat 3 cups oil in a large skillet to 375°F; a cube of bread tossed in will brown quickly. Deep-fry the pastries 4 or 5 at a time until golden. Remove with a slotted spoon. Transfer to a paper-towel-lined platter. Serve hot or at room temperature.

Makes about 30 pastries.

MOROCCO

Filo Pastry Pie with Chicken
(Bastella)

BASTELLA IS A FESTIVE PASTRY of delicate filo filled with savory chicken, eggs and spices and decorated with confectioners' sugar and cinnamon. I first ate this dish in a Moroccan restaurant in Hollywood long before I met my husband and was amazed by the complexity of the flavors. It is a little tricky to assemble the first time, especially if you are not used to working with filo dough.

2	tablespoons vegetable oil	8	large eggs, beaten
1	2-to-3-pound chicken, cut into pieces	¼	cup sugar
	Salt and pepper to taste	2	cups almonds, toasted and ground
1	medium onion, chopped	½	teaspoon cinnamon, plus more for sprinkling
2	cups chicken broth	7	filo dough sheets
1	cinnamon stick	4	tablespoons (½ stick) margarine, melted
	Pinch of saffron threads		Confectioners' sugar for sprinkling
½	cup chopped fresh parsley		
½	cup chopped fresh cilantro		

In a large skillet, heat the oil over medium-high heat, add the chicken and brown for about 5 minutes. Sprinkle with salt and pepper. Add the onion and broth and bring to a boil. Add the cinnamon stick and saffron. Reduce the heat to low and simmer for 1 hour. Remove the chicken with a slotted spoon and set aside to cool. Discard the cinnamon stick and reserve the liquid. Remove the skin and bones from the chicken and shred the meat.

Measure 1 cup of the liquid and return it to the skillet. Add the parsley and cilantro. Simmer, uncovered, for 3 minutes. Stir in the beaten eggs and cook until they are scrambled and the liquid has been absorbed. Remove from the heat and set aside.

Combine the sugar, almonds and ½ teaspoon cinnamon in a small bowl.

Preheat the oven to 300°F, with a rack in the middle.

Grease a 10-inch cake pan or ovenproof skillet. Place 4 sheets of the filo in the bottom of the pan, letting the sheets hang 4 to 5 inches over the sides of the pan. (Cover the remaining filo sheets with a damp dish towel so they will not dry out.) Brush with the melted margarine. Sprinkle a third of the almond mixture over the filo. Spread with half of the shredded chicken, then sprinkle with another third of the almond mixture. Drain the eggs of any excess liquid and spread half of them over the almond mixture. Spread the remaining chicken mixture over it, followed by the remaining egg mixture and ending with the remaining almond mixture. Fold the overhanging filo sheets over the top. Brush with melted margarine. Cover the top with the remaining 3 filo sheets, brushing melted margarine between the sheets. Tuck the overhang under. Bake for about 25 minutes, or until golden on top.

Cool slightly, then invert onto a platter. Sprinkle with the confectioners' sugar and cinnamon. Cut into wedges and serve.

Serves 6 to 8.

Soups

Recipes

GREECE
Egg-Lemon Soup
(Avgolemono)

THIS TRADITIONAL SOUP is served in many Sephardic communities at the end of Yom Kippur to break the fast. The trick is to add the egg mixture gradually to the soup. Do so very slowly and carefully, or the eggs will cook too fast, becoming egg shreds rather than smoothly incorporating into the broth.

8 cups chicken broth	2 teaspoons cornstarch, dissolved in 2 teaspoons water
½ cup long-grain white rice, well rinsed	Salt and white pepper
2 large eggs	1 tablespoon finely chopped fresh parsley or dill for garnish
Juice from 2 lemons, plus more to taste	

Bring the chicken broth to a boil in a large saucepan. Add the rice and cook until tender, about 15 minutes.

In a medium bowl, beat the eggs and then beat in the lemon juice. Scoop out a cup of hot soup and add it, a tablespoon at a time, to the egg mixture, stirring constantly.

Pour the egg-and-soup mixture back into the pot and reduce the heat to low. Simmer just until the soup thickens, about 10 minutes. For a thicker soup, add the cornstarch with water at this point. Be very careful not to increase the heat, or the eggs will curdle. Adjust the seasonings, adding salt and white pepper to taste and lemon juice if needed.

Serve immediately, garnished with the parsley or dill.

Serves 4 to 6.

Yemen
Yemenite Soup

Colored bright yellow by the generous addition of turmeric, this soup is a traditional Jewish cure-all: penicillin for the soul. Yemenites add *zhoug* (hot spicy sauce) to it before serving. Serve the soup with Yemenite Flatbread (page 56).

1 3-pound chicken, cut into 8 pieces, or 1 pound London broil, cut into 6 pieces	2 tablespoons cumin
	2 teaspoons turmeric
	1 teaspoon pepper
1 large tomato, peeled and quartered, or 1 tablespoon tomato paste	Salt to taste
8 garlic cloves, minced	4 medium white boiling potatoes, peeled and quartered
8 sprigs parsley	1 tablespoon all-purpose flour
8 sprigs fresh cilantro	1 tablespoon cold water

Bring 10 cups water to a boil in a large pot. Add the chicken or beef, tomato, garlic, parsley, cilantro, cumin, turmeric, pepper and salt. Reduce the heat to low and simmer for 45 minutes.

If using chicken, strain the soup through a colander into a large bowl. Remove and discard the bones and skin from the chicken. Return the soup, including the chicken or beef, to the pot.

Add the potatoes and continue simmering for 15 minutes, or until tender.

Mix the flour with the cold water in a small cup and mix until it forms a smooth paste. Add a little hot soup to the flour in the cup to dilute the flour paste, then whisk the flour paste into the soup and continue cooking for 15 minutes, or until the soup has a little more body. Skim the fat off the top using a ladle or large spoon and serve.

Serves 4 to 6.

SYRIA
Thick Rice Soup
(Shurba)

THIS THICK TOMATO-RICE SOUP is a staple throughout the Middle East. A simple, hearty, nutritious soup, it is a meal in itself, especially with the meatballs.

4	lean, meaty lamb shanks
6	medium tomatoes, peeled and chopped, or 3 cups canned chopped tomatoes
1	medium onion, finely chopped
½	teaspoon nutmeg
2	teaspoons salt
½	teaspoon pepper
½	cup long-grain white rice
1½	tablespoons tomato paste

Meatballs (Optional)

½	pound ground beef
½	teaspoon cinnamon
½	teaspoon allspice
½	teaspoon salt
2	tablespoons raw long-grain white rice

Bring 8 cups water to a boil in a soup pot and add the lamb shanks. Reduce the heat to medium and simmer, uncovered, for 2½ hours, skimming the top occasionally with a ladle to remove the froth. Remove the bones and add 8 more cups water. Stir in the tomatoes, onion, nutmeg, salt and pepper. Reduce the heat to low and simmer, covered, for 30 minutes. Add the rice and simmer until tender, about 15 minutes. Stir in the tomato paste. If the soup is to be served without meatballs, simmer for 10 to 15 minutes more before serving.

To make the meatballs (optional): Combine all the ingredients in a medium bowl, shape into 1-inch balls and add to the boiling soup. Simmer for about 30 minutes more to cook the meatballs.

Adjust the seasonings, adding salt and pepper if needed, and serve.

Serves 6 to 8.

SYRIA

Syrian Sour Soup

(Hamud)

MY ELDER DAUGHTER, Satya, fell in love with this tangy vegetable soup, which is traditionally considered a sauce, because her friend's grandmother, Leona Fallas, prepared it as a Friday-night ritual. When I received the recipe, I thought it looked a little dull and I filed it away. After much prodding from my daughter, I finally made it. It has a wonderful flavor and makes a great vegetarian meal with rice. Traditionally, however, it is used as a sauce for meatballs and served over rice.

The meatballs use rice flour, which is available in Middle Eastern and Indian markets. If you can't find it, substitute the meatballs in Thick Rice Soup (page 80).

1 large boiling potato, peeled and cubed	**Meatballs**
2 celery stalks, diced	1 pound lean ground beef (ground turkey can be substituted)
1 bunch parsley, chopped	¾ cup rice flour
1 bunch green onions (about 6), chopped	½ teaspoon salt
2-4 garlic cloves	
½ teaspoon kosher salt	
2 small zucchini, peeled and diced	
Juice from 2 lemons	
2 teaspoons crushed fresh mint leaves	

In a medium pot, bring 4 cups water, the potato, celery, parsley and green onions to a boil. Reduce the heat to low and simmer for 15 minutes. Meanwhile, crush the garlic and salt with a mortar and pestle or in a small bowl with a fork and add to the vegetables. Add the zucchini, lemon juice and mint. Simmer for 10 to 15 minutes, or until the vegetables are cooked and the flavors have been absorbed into the broth.

Meanwhile, make the meatballs: Grind the beef and rice flour together in a food processor into a firm mixture. Add the salt. Break off pieces of the mixture, roll them into small balls about ¾ inch in diameter and flatten them into small flat disks about 1½ to 2 inches in diameter. Add the meatballs to the soup, cover and continue cooking for 15 minutes, or until they are cooked through. Serve hot over rice.

Serves 6, with about 3 cups broth.

LEBANON
Lentil and Meatball Soup

THIS HEARTY, NUTRITIOUS SOUP is enhanced by savory meatballs. It was inspired by a recipe given to me by Helena, the first Sephardic woman I ever knew. I remember sitting in her kitchen as a teenager when she explained that her family had originally come from Spain in the 15th century. At that time, I thought it odd to know where your ancestors were from. But knowledge of one's distant roots is common among the Sephardic Jews I have met since.

¾ pound (about 2 cups) brown lentils	2 large carrots, peeled and diced
1 pound lean ground beef	2 celery stalks with leaves, diced
1 teaspoon salt	2 cups chopped onion
¼ teaspoon pepper	1 14-ounce can tomato sauce
⅛ teaspoon allspice	5 cups chicken broth or warm water
⅛ teaspoon cinnamon	1 garlic clove, minced
¼ cup vegetable oil	1 tablespoon chopped fresh parsley

Wash the lentils in cold water and pick out any small stones or discolored lentils; drain and set aside.

Combine the ground beef with the salt, pepper, allspice and cinnamon in a medium bowl. Roll into tiny balls ½ inch or less in diameter.

Heat the oil in a soup pot. Add the meatballs and brown in batches over high heat for 5 to 7 minutes, gently turning to brown evenly. Remove the meatballs with a slotted spoon and

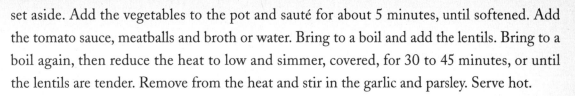

set aside. Add the vegetables to the pot and sauté for about 5 minutes, until softened. Add the tomato sauce, meatballs and broth or water. Bring to a boil and add the lentils. Bring to a boil again, then reduce the heat to low and simmer, covered, for 30 to 45 minutes, or until the lentils are tender. Remove from the heat and stir in the garlic and parsley. Serve hot.

Serves 6.

IRAQ

Sweet-and-Sour Pumpkin Soup with Meatballs

HILE I WAS LIVING WITH MY IN-LAWS IN 1987, I attended an intensive course in Hebrew during the day. I would come home at lunchtime to find that my mother-in-law had prepared a delicious meal. If I raved about a certain dish, she remembered and prepared it often. One of my favorites was this sweet-and-sour soup that contains pumpkin and meatballs. The raw rice, which is added to the meatballs, softens as the meatballs cook and makes them lighter.

Meatballs

1   pound ground beef

½   teaspoon cinnamon

½   teaspoon salt

½   teaspoon allspice

2   tablespoons raw long-grain white rice

Soup

4   teaspoons vegetable oil

2   medium onions, finely chopped

1   medium green pepper, finely chopped

2   pounds pumpkin, peeled and cut into 2-inch cubes

Juice from 2 large lemons

3   tablespoons tomato paste

10 cups chicken broth or water

1   cup dried apricots, 1 cup pitted dried prunes, or ½ cup seedless dark raisins (optional)

1   heaping tablespoon sugar (if dried fruit is not used)

Salt and pepper to taste

To make the meatballs: Combine all the ingredients and shape the mixture into 1-inch balls. Cover with a clean dish towel while preparing the soup.

To make the soup: In a heavy pot, heat the oil over medium heat and sauté the onions until transparent, about 5 minutes. Add the green pepper and pumpkin and cook until slightly softened, about 5 minutes. Add the lemon juice, tomato paste and chicken broth or water. Bring to a boil. If using the dried fruit, add it at this point and reduce the heat to low.

Cook, covered, over low heat for 20 minutes, stirring occasionally. Add the meatballs. Cover and cook for 20 minutes more, or until the meatballs are cooked through. Adjust the seasonings, adding sugar if you didn't use the dried fruit, and salt and pepper. Serve hot.

Serves 6.

Okra Stew with Stuffed Dumplings
(Kubbah Bamyah)

THE MENTION of *kubbah bamyah* will bring a glow of recognition to almost any Jew of Iraqi heritage. *Kubbah* is a stuffed dumpling, a bit like the European *kreplach* but heavier. *Bamyah*, or okra, is a much-loved vegetable in the Middle East, and this sweet-and-sour okra stew with dumplings has become a favorite combination in my home. Semolina is sold in Middle Eastern or specialty shops in the pasta section.

Dumpling Filling

- 3 tablespoons finely chopped onion
- 1 tablespoon olive oil
- 1 pound ground beef, lamb or chicken
- 3 tablespoons minced fresh parsley
- 3 tablespoons minced celery leaves
- Dash of salt and pepper

Dumpling Shell

- 2½ cups semolina
- ½ teaspoon salt
- About 1¾ cups water

Okra Stew

- 2 pounds small okra, about 3 inches long
- 2 tablespoons white vinegar
- 3 tablespoons olive oil
- 1 28-ounce can (2 cups) peeled tomatoes, drained and chopped
- 2 quarts water or chicken broth
- 3 tablespoons tomato paste
- ¾ cup lemon juice
- 2 tablespoons sugar
- 1 teaspoon salt
- Pepper

To make the dumpling filling: In a medium skillet, sauté the onion in the oil until translucent, about 3 minutes. Add the ground meat and cook until the meat is no longer pink, about 5 minutes, breaking up the larger pieces with a fork. Stir in the parsley, celery leaves and salt and pepper. Cover and cook for a few more minutes; the meat should be fully cooked. Remove from the heat and set aside to cool.

To make the dumpling shell: Combine the semolina and salt in a medium bowl. Add enough water to form a stiff but pliable dough. Divide the dough into 18 balls the size of walnuts. Puncture each ball with your finger and fill with 1 tablespoon filling. Pinch the opening closed. Flatten the ball into a disk about 3 inches wide, using the palms of your hands. Continue until all dough is used. Cover and refrigerate until ready to use.

To make the okra stew: Wash the okra and trim the stems without cutting into the vegetable. Cover the okra with hot water and add the vinegar. Set aside for 30 minutes. Drain. Pat dry with a clean dish towel.

Heat the oil and sauté the okra over medium-high heat until lightly browned on all sides, about 15 minutes. Add the tomatoes and cook until the liquid has evaporated. Add the water or chicken broth, bring to a boil and stir in the tomato paste, lemon juice, sugar and salt. Cover and simmer for 30 minutes. Add the dumplings and continue cooking for 20 minutes more to fully cook them. Before serving, adjust the seasonings, adding salt and pepper to taste. Serve hot.

Serves 4 to 6; makes 18 dumplings.

IRAQ
Beet Soup with Stuffed Dumplings
(Kubbah Adom)

HEN YACOV'S AUNT HAVAH AND AUNT RENE visited from Israel, I told them I was collecting recipes for a book. Havah said that Rene was the best cook in the family and that she should give me the recipe for *kubbah adom*. I had cooked this dish for 10 years, but out of respect, I listened. As Rene began to recite the recipe, everyone present began to argue about how much of this or that was used, with both aunts finally admitting that they never measured. An hour and a half later, I had the same basic recipe I had started with.

5	beets (about 1½ pounds), peeled	1	tablespoon sugar
3	tablespoons vegetable oil		Salt and pepper to taste
1	medium onion, finely chopped		
6	cups water	1	recipe Stuffed Dumplings
3	tablespoons tomato paste		(page 88)
¼	cup lemon juice		

Boil the beets for 10 minutes, until slightly softened. Drain and let cool. When the beets are at room temperature, grate them coarsely using a food processor or hand grater.

Heat the oil in a soup pot over medium heat and sauté the onion for about 3 minutes, or until translucent. Add the beets and continue sautéing for 2 to 3 minutes more. Stir in the water and tomato paste. Simmer, uncovered, for 15 minutes, then stir in the lemon juice, sugar and salt and pepper. Cook for 5 minutes to allow the flavors to blend, then bring to a boil and gently drop in the stuffed dumplings. Cover, reduce the heat to low and simmer for 20 minutes, or until the dumplings are cooked through.

To serve, transfer the dumplings with a slotted spoon to individual soup bowls and spoon the beets and soup around the stuffed dumplings.

Serves 6; makes 18 dumplings.

IRAN
Chicken Soup with Chickpea Meatballs
(Ghondi)

GHONDI, THE IRANIAN EQUIVALENT of the European matzo ball, is a combination of ground meat and chickpea flour molded into flavorful balls that embellish chicken soup or rice dishes. This recipe was given to me by the grandmother of a friend of my daughter. It is important to make more than enough for dinner, because leftover *ghondi* balls are also traditionally eaten cold on Shabbat morning with pita bread, green vegetables and radishes. Roasted chickpea flour is available in Middle Eastern and Persian markets.

Chicken Broth		Chickpea Meatballs	
10	cups water	1	pound ground chicken or beef
1	4-pound chicken, cut into pieces	2	cups roasted chickpea flour
2	onions, coarsely chopped	2	onions, minced
2	carrots, halved	1	teaspoon cardamom
3	celery stalks with leaves	1	teaspoon cumin
1	bunch parsley	1	teaspoon turmeric
1	turnip, quartered	1	teaspoon salt
1½	teaspoons salt	½	teaspoon pepper
1	teaspoon pepper	¼	cup vegetable oil or melted
1	teaspoon turmeric		chicken fat

To make the chicken broth: Combine all the ingredients in a large soup pot. Bring to a boil and simmer for 2 hours, or until the chicken pulls away from the bones. Strain the broth into a container, reserving the meat for a separate purpose and discarding the vegetables. Refrigerate the broth. Before using, skim the fat off the top.

To make the chickpea meatballs: Mix together all the ingredients and shape into meatballs the size of small limes.

Bring the chicken broth to a simmer. Gently place each meatball into the broth. Cover and cook over medium heat for 20 minutes. Serve the meatballs hot in the chicken soup and/or with rice.

Serves 6.

Tunisia
Passover Lamb Stew
(Msoki)

HEN WE LIVED IN LOS ANGELES, we threw large dinner parties, converting our living room into a dining room. We moved everything out, with the exception of the baby grand piano, and set the room with two nine-foot folding tables side by side, creating a huge rectangular table that seated 32. With all my culinary friends, events like these were easy because everyone brought preassigned dishes.

One of the most memorable of these parties was a Passover dinner in 1991. Evelyne and David Guez brought *msoki*, a thick Tunisian lamb stew that is traditionally eaten during the week of Passover. It has since become one of my favorites. The lamb is symbolic of the Pascal sacrifice used for the Exodus, and the vegetables represent the advent of the new season. Matzos are crumbled into the stew before serving.

½ cup vegetable oil

3 pounds lamb shanks

4 large carrots, peeled and cubed

3 large boiling potatoes, peeled and cubed

3 medium turnips, peeled and cubed

4 fresh or frozen artichoke hearts, quartered

2 fennel heads, base quartered, stalks chopped

1 small cabbage, chopped

1 small cauliflower, cut into florets

3 celery stalks, cut into 2-inch pieces

2 medium onions, sliced

6 garlic cloves, chopped

2 medium leeks, cut into 2-inch pieces

2 pounds fresh fava beans, pods removed but skins left on

1 pound fresh or frozen peas

2 pounds fresh spinach, washed and chopped

1	large zucchini, cubed	2	teaspoons salt
4	tablespoons tomato paste	1	teaspoon allspice
½	cup chopped fresh dill	1	teaspoon pepper
½	cup chopped fresh parsley	1	teaspoon white pepper
½	cup chopped fresh cilantro	1	cinnamon stick
10	mint leaves	6	matzos, broken into pieces
2	teaspoons nutmeg		

Heat ¼ cup of the oil in a large soup pot. Add the lamb shanks and fry in batches over medium-high heat for about 6 minutes, turning to brown on all sides. (If you wish to serve the shanks whole rather than having the meat fall off the bones, remove them now and set aside.) Pour in enough water to cover the meat by 2 inches and simmer, uncovered, for 1½ hours, occasionally skimming off any froth.

In a separate deep pot, heat the remaining ¼ cup oil. Add the carrots, potatoes, turnips and artichoke hearts and sauté for 5 minutes, then transfer to the soup pot. Add the fennel, cabbage, cauliflower, celery, onion and garlic to the second pot and sauté for 5 minutes, then transfer to the soup pot. Add the leeks, fava beans, peas, spinach and zucchini to the second pot and sauté for 5 minutes, then transfer to the soup pot. Add enough water to cover all the ingredients.

Bring to a boil, reduce the heat to low, cover and simmer for 1 hour. Stir in the tomato paste, herbs and spices and continue cooking for 30 minutes to blend the flavors. (Return the shanks to the pot, if you removed them earlier.) When they are hot, take them out with a slotted spoon and serve on a separate plate.

Serve the soup hot in bowls, crumbling the matzos on top.

Serves 10.

Morocco
Moroccan Couscous

WHEN A NORTH AFRICAN INVITES YOU OVER FOR COUSCOUS, it will be much more than the pasta. The meal consists of various *mezze* dishes of marinated vegetables, followed by the couscous served with a rich vegetable and meat broth. Traditionally, couscous is prepared in a tall double pot called a *couscousier*, which has a bottom pot for the broth and vegetables and a steamer above for the pasta.

Moroccans prepare couscous in a variety of ways, with chicken, beef, lamb, fish or milk and butter. It can be sweet—prepared with pumpkin, onions, raisins, prunes, sugar and cinnamon—or savory, with vegetables and meat broth. The recipe given here is a basic savory version.

4 tablespoons vegetable oil, plus a little more for drizzling over the vegetables	10 cups water
	½ cabbage head, halved
2 medium onions, quartered	1 pound red squash (banana squash) or pumpkin
2 pounds lamb shoulder or London broil, cut into 3-to-4-inch pieces	2 cups canned chickpeas (garbanzo beans)
½ teaspoon turmeric	4 medium zucchini, about 8 inches long, cut into large chunks
Salt and pepper to taste	
4 large carrots, peeled and halved	1 pound (2¾ cups) uncooked couscous
2 medium white turnips, peeled and cut into chunks	1 teaspoon brown sugar
3 celery stalks, cut into thirds	1 teaspoon cinnamon

Heat 3 tablespoons of the oil in a deep pot. Add the onions and the meat; sauté over medium-high heat for 5 to 10 minutes, until browned. Add the turmeric, salt and pepper. Add the carrots, turnips, celery and water and simmer for 1 hour. Add the cabbage, squash and chickpeas and simmer for 1 hour more. Drain the vegetables, reserving the broth; keep it warm on the stovetop. Transfer the vegetables to an ovenproof serving dish, leaving the meat in the broth.

Place the couscous in a large bowl. Add enough water to dampen but not drown it. Wait until the water has been absorbed. Work the couscous with your fingers, opening and loosening the granules. Moisten the couscous again and sprinkle with salt. Place the couscous in a steamer over the pot to steam above the broth for 10 minutes. Remove the granules and cool in a large bowl. Gently loosen the granules with your fingers or a fork. Add the remaining 1 tablespoon oil to the couscous. Steam again for 20 minutes and keep warm. (The couscous can be reheated in a microwave oven.)

Drizzle a little oil over the vegetables and sprinkle the brown sugar and cinnamon over them. Preheat the broiler, with a rack about 5 inches from the heat. Broil the vegetables until golden, about 3 minutes.

Divide the couscous among 8 bowls and top with vegetables and meat. Ladle broth generously into each bowl. Serve hot.

Serves 8.

Tunisian Couscous

HEN I FIRST BEGAN MY VENTURES into North African cuisine, I thought all couscous was alike. I did not realize that there were so many differences in the ways cooks served this dish. While Moroccans prefer a sweet-tasting couscous, Tunisians like more savory flavors.

The meat is cut into pieces larger than stewing beef because there are meant to be some good-sized chunks for serving even after long cooking. The vegetables are halved, with the exception of the turnips, which are quartered so they can be distinguished after cooking from the potatoes.

Serve this delicious dish with Tunisian Meatballs (page 162) on the side.

2 tablespoons vegetable oil	1 15-ounce can chickpeas (garbanzo beans), drained
2-3 pounds London broil, cut into 4-inch cubes	3 zucchini, about 6 inches long, cut into 3-inch chunks
3 medium carrots, peeled and halved	3 sprigs fresh parsley or cilantro
2 celery stalks, cut into thirds	¾ teaspoon turmeric, or to taste
1-2 turnips, peeled and quartered	¾ teaspoon allspice, or to taste
2 medium leeks, cut into 2-inch pieces	¾ teaspoon salt, or to taste
1 onion, quartered	¾ teaspoon pepper, or to taste
1 large tomato, peeled and quartered	*Harissa* (hot pepper sauce), optional
2 beef marrow bones (optional)	1 pound (2¾ cups) uncooked couscous
3 medium boiling potatoes, peeled and halved	
½ cabbage, halved	Tunisian Meatballs (page 162)

In a large soup pot, heat 1 tablespoon of the oil over medium heat. Add the beef in batches and brown on all sides, about 3 minutes per batch, setting aside in a bowl after browning. Add the carrots, celery, turnips, leeks, onion and tomato to the soup pot and sauté until tender, about 10 minutes. Return the beef to the pot and add enough water to cover the vegetables and meat by 1 inch. Add the marrow bones, if using, and simmer for 2 hours. Add the potatoes, cabbage and chickpeas, cover and continue cooking for 30 minutes. Add the zucchini, parsley or cilantro and spices, including the *harissa*, if desired.

Put the couscous in a large bowl. Add enough water to dampen but not drown it. Wait until the water has been absorbed. Work the couscous with your fingers, opening and loosening the granules. Moisten the couscous again and sprinkle with salt. Place the couscous in a steamer over the pot to steam above the broth for 10 minutes. Remove the granules and cool in a large bowl. Gently loosen the granules with your fingers or a fork. Add the remaining 1 tablespoon oil to the couscous. Steam again for 20 minutes and keep warm. (The couscous can be reheated in a microwave oven.)

Adjust the seasonings of the broth, adding more turmeric, salt, pepper and allspice to taste.

Divide the couscous among 8 bowls and ladle the broth, meat and vegetables together from the pot, spooning them over the couscous. Serve with Tunisian Meatballs on the side.

Serves 8.

Fish

Recipes

LEBANON
Baked Fish in Tahina Sauce

MANY YEARS AGO, when I was first learning about Sephardic food, I arranged for a group of friends, each with a mastery of her own culinary traditions, to form a cooking class. A wonderful cook named Sophie Saayed demonstrated the preparation of this simple fish, which is baked and covered with tahina sauce. For decoration, the fish is covered with lemon slices like scales, with a pine nut placed in the eye cavity. Pomegranate seeds are sometimes used in place of lemon slices.

1 **2-pound fish, cleaned, scaled and left whole, preferably with the head attached**	1 **medium onion, chopped**
1 **tablespoon salt**	1 **cup Tahina (page 38)**
4 **tablespoons olive oil**	**Chopped fresh parsley, lemon slices and a pine nut for garnish**

Sprinkle the fish with the salt inside and out and refrigerate for 1 hour. Let the fish return to room temperature before cooking. Preheat the oven to 350°F.

Place the fish in a 9-by-13-inch baking dish and rub with 1 tablespoon of the oil. Bake for 8 minutes per inch of thickness.

Sauté the onion in the remaining 3 tablespoons oil over medium heat until transparent, about 4 minutes. Stir the tahina into the onion. Pour the mixture over the fish and return to the oven to cook for 15 minutes more, or until the fish flakes easily when tested with a fork.

Garnish the fish with parsley and lemon slices. Place a pine nut in the eye cavity. Serve hot or cold.

Serves 4.

INDIA
Baked Fish with Coriander

THIS STUFFED FISH IS DELICIOUSLY PUNGENT with Indian flavors. To get the fish from the oven to the platter without breaking it, line a greased baking dish with a double thickness of aluminum foil, allowing the foil to extend past the edges of the dish on both sides. Grease the foil, place the fish on it and bake as directed. When the fish is done, remove it from the oven and use the foil handles to transfer the fish from the baking dish to the serving platter. Serve with Basmati Rice Pilaf (page 193).

1	4-pound firm white fish, cleaned, scaled and left whole	1	teaspoon molasses
1½	teaspoons salt	1	teaspoon turmeric
2	tablespoons plus ½ cup olive oil	½	teaspoon fenugreek seeds
½	cup lemon juice	2	cups finely chopped onion
4	tablespoons chopped fresh cilantro	1	cup finely chopped peeled and seeded tomatoes
3	tablespoons finely chopped garlic	½	teaspoon garam masala (Indian spice mixture, found in Indian markets or other specialty shops)
2	tablespoons peeled and minced fresh ginger		
1	tablespoon coriander seeds		

Preheat the oven to 400°F, with a rack in the middle.

Prepare a 9-by-13-inch baking dish. Wash the fish under cold water. Pat dry. Sprinkle the inside with 1 teaspoon of the salt. Set aside while preparing the stuffing.

In a blender or a food processor fitted with the metal blade, combine 2 tablespoons of the oil, the lemon juice, 2 tablespoons of the cilantro, garlic, ginger, coriander seeds, molasses, turmeric, fenugreek and the remaining ½ teaspoon salt. Blend on high, scraping down the sides until the mixture is a smooth puree.

In a large heavy skillet, heat the remaining ½ cup oil, add the onion, and cook over medium heat, stirring, until golden brown, 5 to 10 minutes. Add the seasoning puree and sauté for about 10 minutes. Stir in the tomatoes and the garam masala and remove from the heat. Coat one side of the fish with the tomato-spice mixture and place, coated side down, in the baking dish. Fill the inside of the fish with 1 cup of the mixture. Sew or skewer the opening closed. Spread the remaining mixture over the top of the fish.

Cover the dish with foil and bake for 35 minutes, or until the fish flakes easily when tested with a fork. Uncover, turn on the broiler and broil for 2 minutes, until lightly browned. Sprinkle with the remaining 2 tablespoons cilantro before serving.

Serves 6 to 8.

IRAQ
Sweet-and-Sour Fish
(Salona)

THIS DISH, fish fillets braised in a rich sweet-and-sour sauce, is served during festive family celebrations or for Shabbat. It can be made on the top of the stove or, as in this recipe, baked in the oven.

2-3 tablespoons vegetable oil	3 pounds white fish fillets, such as red snapper or grouper
2 medium onions, sliced	½ cup lemon juice
2 green peppers, sliced	1 heaping tablespoon tomato paste
1 hot green pepper, sliced	2 tablespoons sugar
6 medium tomatoes, sliced	¼ teaspoon turmeric
3 garlic cloves, thinly sliced	2 tablespoons finely chopped fresh cilantro or parsley (optional)
½ teaspoon salt	
½ teaspoon pepper	

Preheat the oven to 350°F.

Heat the oil in a large heavy pot and sauté the onions over medium-high heat until they are golden brown and have begun to lose their moisture, 5 to 10 minutes. Remove with a slotted spoon and place in an even layer in a 9-by-13-inch nonreactive baking dish.

Sauté the peppers in the pot over medium-high heat for 2 minutes, or until slightly softened. With a slotted spoon, transfer them to the baking dish, layering them over the onions. Place half of the tomato slices on top of the peppers, followed by a sprinkling of the garlic. Season with the salt and pepper.

In the pot used for the vegetables, sauté the fish fillets for 1 minute on each side, then transfer them to the baking dish. Top the fish with the remaining tomato slices.

Combine the lemon juice, tomato paste, sugar and turmeric in a small bowl and mix until smooth. Pour over the top layer. Sprinkle with cilantro or parsley, if using. Cover with foil and bake for 20 minutes. Remove the foil and bake for 10 minutes more, or until the fish flakes easily when tested with a fork. Serve immediately.

Serves 6 to 8.

RHODES

Baked Fish in Tomato Sauce
(Peskado kon Salsa de Tomat)

BECAUSE RHODES IS AN ISLAND, fresh fish is plentiful and is always included in a festive meal. Rebecca Levy, a Rhodes native, describes the fish-preparation options for Shabbat: "One week you fry it, another week you might make it with tomatoes and onions, then the next week you can make it with a sour lemon sauce." The following recipe incorporates tomatoes, onions, lemon juice and parsley. The addition of white wine is probably a modern adaptation.

1	3-pound sea bass or other firm white fish, filleted	1	cup canned tomatoes, drained and chopped
2	medium onions, chopped	½	cup dry white wine
¼	cup chopped fresh parsley	½	cup tomato juice
1	large garlic clove, minced	¼	cup lemon juice
	Salt and pepper to taste	2	tablespoons olive oil

Preheat the oven to 350°F. Grease a 9-by-13-inch baking dish.

Place the fish in the baking dish. Sprinkle the onion, parsley, garlic, salt and pepper over the fish. Cover with the tomatoes. Sprinkle the wine, tomato juice, lemon juice and olive oil over the top.

Bake for 30 minutes, or until the fish flakes easily when tested with a fork. Serve immediately.

Serves 6.

TUNISIA
Fish H'raimi

MY FRIEND JACO HALFON, who is from Tunisia, told me that this fish was called *h'raimi*, sly, because the spicy sauce disguises the fishy taste of the original dish. It is sly in another way too: the wonderful sauce looks and tastes as if it was prepared with great care for hours, but in fact, it is a quick recipe.

¼ cup olive oil	2 pounds tuna steaks, ½-¾ inch thick
6 garlic cloves, minced	½ cup cold water
Juice from 1 lemon	1 tablespoon bread crumbs
1 teaspoon paprika	2 tablespoons chopped fresh
½ teaspoon *harissa* (hot pepper sauce)	chives or cilantro for garnish
½ teaspoon tomato paste	

In a saucepan large enough to hold the fish in a single layer, heat the oil and sauté the garlic over medium-high heat until softened, about 3 minutes. Stir in the lemon juice, paprika, *harissa* and tomato paste. Add the fish. Add the cold water; it will almost cover the fish. Bring to a boil, then reduce the heat to low and simmer for 8 minutes, or until the fish flakes easily when tested with a fork. Remove from the heat, stir in the bread crumbs and cover the pan. Let cool slightly. Garnish with the chives or cilantro. Serve warm or cold with bread.

Serves 4.

Iran
Herb-Stuffed Fish

THE MOST IMPORTANT CONCEPT in Persian cuisine is to know and expect that every meal is going to be a feast, at least by American standards. Generally several dishes are served on platters simultaneously, and dining is expected to last for hours.

A fish course is always part of a Jewish celebration, but in our modern lifestyles, fish can also be a main dish. The following recipe brings together some of the many herbs used in Persian cooking. Serve with rice.

4 pounds trout, orange roughy or other firm white fish, left whole and cleaned	½ cup chopped fresh parsley
	4 tablespoons chopped fresh tarragon
	2 tablespoons chopped fresh mint
Salt	¼ cup lemon juice
1 teaspoon olive oil	½ teaspoon pepper
2 garlic cloves, chopped	¼ teaspoon turmeric

Sprinkle the fish inside and out with salt. Preheat the oven to 350°F.

Heat the oil in a large nonstick pan and sauté the garlic over medium-high heat until golden, about 3 minutes. Add all the herbs and sauté until they are wilted, about 2 minutes. Fill the fish with the herb mixture and sew the cavity closed, using a needle and thread or toothpicks.

Line a 9-by-13-inch baking dish with double layers of aluminum foil, allowing enough foil overhang on each side of the dish to wrap back over and seal the fish in a package. Place the fish in the middle of the foil-lined dish.

Pour the lemon juice over the fish and sprinkle with 1 teaspoon salt, pepper and turmeric. Bring the foil together and fold the edges over, sealing the fish inside.

Bake for 30 to 45 minutes, or until the fish flakes easily when tested with a fork. Serve immediately.

Serves 6.

Baked Fish with Chickpeas

HIS MOROCCAN-STYLE FISH is seasoned with aromatic spices. Tomatoes, peppers, chickpeas and olives add to the Mediterranean flair. If you are serving roasted peppers and tomatoes as a *mezze*, you may want to consider leaving them out of this dish. It tastes just as good without them.

½ cup vegetable oil	1 cup canned chickpeas (garbanzo beans), drained
2 tablespoons lemon juice	2 large tomatoes, sliced
½ cup finely chopped fresh cilantro	1 green pepper, seeded and cut into thin strips
1 tablespoon turmeric	5 garlic cloves, chopped
1 tablespoon cumin	2 small hot red peppers, chopped (optional)
1 tablespoon paprika	12-20 brine-cured black olives, such as kalamata
3 pounds trout, halibut, orange roughy or other firm white fish fillets	
1 large onion, sliced	

In a large bowl, whisk together the oil, lemon juice, cilantro, turmeric, cumin and paprika. Add the fish fillets and turn to coat both sides with the marinade. Refrigerate for 1 to 2 hours.

Preheat the oven to 375°F.

Place the onion slices, then the chickpeas, in the bottom of a 9-by-13-inch baking dish. Place the fish fillets on top. Cover with the tomato slices and pepper strips.

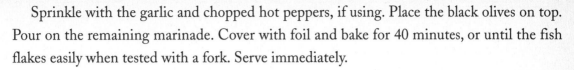

Sprinkle with the garlic and chopped hot peppers, if using. Place the black olives on top. Pour on the remaining marinade. Cover with foil and bake for 40 minutes, or until the fish flakes easily when tested with a fork. Serve immediately.

Serves 6.

Yemenite Fish

GOT THIS RECIPE OVER DINNER AT A BAR MITZVAH, where I was sitting next to a woman who was from Yemen. After a brief introduction, I immediately started to question her about the food she prepared. I jotted down the recipe on an envelope from my purse and have been making it for my family ever since.

This spicy, yellow-tinted fish can be served as a first course or as a main dish with rice, flatbread and *zhoug* (page 255), if you like fiery condiments. The seasoning base, *hawaji*, is similar to Indian garam masala or curry powder.

Hawaji Seasoning	Fish
1 tablespoon pepper	2 pounds sole or halibut fillets
2 teaspoons turmeric	1 teaspoon salt
2 teaspoons salt	1 teaspoon cumin
1 teaspoon caraway seeds	1 teaspoon turmeric
1 teaspoon cardamom seeds	¼ teaspoon pepper
1 teaspoon saffron threads	½ cup all-purpose flour
	Vegetable oil or olive oil for frying

To make the *hawaji* seasoning: Pound all the ingredients in a mortar or spice grinder. Set aside. The mixture can be made ahead and stored in an airtight container for up to 6 months.

To make the fish: Rinse the fish and pat dry. Combine the *hawaji* seasoning, salt, cumin, turmeric and pepper in a shallow dish. Dip the fish fillets in the seasoning mixture, coating both sides. Set aside for several minutes to allow the spices to permeate the fish.

Place the flour in a second shallow dish. Dredge each fish fillet in the flour, coating both sides.

In a large deep skillet, heat the oil. Sauté the fish over medium heat until lightly browned, about 1 minute, then gently turn the fillets and cook the other side. Serve immediately.

Serves 4.

Chicken

Recipes

MOROCCO

Chicken with Olives

THIS IS MY HUSBAND'S FAVORITE DISH. He loves to tell everyone how simple it is to make, which I find rather annoying, since he has never prepared it. Nevertheless, it *is* very easy and tastes even better the next day—handy when you are planning a dinner party. Do not add salt, because the olives are very salty. Serve with white rice or couscous.

5 garlic cloves, chopped	½ teaspoon pepper
¼ cup olive oil	1 pound pitted green
2 medium tomatoes, chopped	Mediterranean-style olives
1 3-pound chicken, cut into	Juice from 1 lemon
8 serving pieces, with	½ cup finely chopped fresh
skin and bones	cilantro leaves
½ teaspoon turmeric	

In a large pot, sauté the garlic in oil over medium heat until golden, about 3 minutes. Add the tomatoes and sauté for 2 to 3 minutes more, until softened. Add the chicken, turmeric and pepper and cook over low heat, uncovered, for 15 minutes, turning occasionally.

Add enough water to almost cover the chicken (about 1 cup), then add the olives. Cover and simmer for about 30 minutes more, or until the chicken is almost tender. Add the lemon juice and cilantro and cook, uncovered, for 15 minutes more. Serve hot.

Serves 4 to 6.

IRAQ

Chicken Stuffed with Rice
(T'bit)

NO OTHER DISH IS QUITE AS DEFINITIVE of the Iraqi Shabbat as *t'bit*. This chicken, stuffed with rice, is cooked within a mound of more rice, heavily laced with cardamom, allspice and cinnamon. Raw eggs in their shells are tucked inside the rice mound. The finished *t'bit* is turned out onto a large platter, and the chicken falls apart into pieces within the rice. Just before serving, the eggs are carefully removed, rinsed and put into a separate bowl. This recipe came from Yacov's cousin Dora Kamara.

1 whole medium-sized chicken (about 3 pounds)	4 teaspoons turmeric
	1 teaspoon salt
	½ teaspoon pepper
Stuffing	4 cups chicken broth
1 medium tomato, chopped	1 6-ounce can tomato sauce
1 chicken gizzard, finely chopped	2 tablespoons allspice
4 tablespoons long-grain white rice	1 tablespoon cardamom
1 teaspoon vegetable oil	Dash each of cinnamon and cloves
Dash each of cinnamon, cardamom, cloves, salt and pepper	
2-3 dried rose petals (optional)	5-6 cups long-grain white rice (preferably basmati)
5 tablespoons vegetable oil	**Brown Roasted Eggs**
2 medium tomatoes, chopped	6 raw eggs in their shells
1 medium onion, chopped	

Rinse the chicken inside and out; pat dry.

To make the stuffing: Combine all the stuffing ingredients. Spoon the mixture into the cavity of the chicken. Using a sterilized needle and thread, sew the loose flaps of skin at the base of the chicken cavity closed.

Heat 1 tablespoon of the oil in a Dutch oven. Add the tomatoes and onion, sautéing over medium-high heat until the onion is golden, about 4 minutes. Add 1 teaspoon of the turmeric, ½ teaspoon of the salt and the pepper.

Place the chicken in the Dutch oven on top of the sautéed mixture. Brown the chicken over medium heat for about 10 minutes on each side, or until golden. Add the broth, tomato sauce, allspice, the remaining 3 teaspoons turmeric, the cardamom, cinnamon, cloves and the remaining ½ teaspoon salt. Bring to a boil and boil for 5 minutes, then reduce the heat to low.

Wash the rice well, draining off the excess water. Spoon the rice around the chicken. Poke the chicken several times to allow some liquid to be absorbed into the cavity. Pour the remaining 4 tablespoons oil around the chicken. Cover and cook on top of the stove until the rice is half-cooked, about 20 minutes.

Preheat the oven to 350°F.

To cook the eggs: Hide the eggs in the rice surrounding the chicken. Add 1 cup water to the rice. Cover the pot with aluminum foil and place the lid on top.

Bake for 30 minutes. Reduce the temperature to 125°F and bake for 6 to 8 hours (or overnight on lowest setting).

Place the eggs in a separate bowl and turn out the rice and chicken onto a large platter.

Serves 6 to 8.

INDIA

Cardamom Chicken

ICHLY SEASONED WITH EXOTIC SPICES, this chicken produces a flavorful sauce from the braising juices. The recipe, shared by a woman from Bombay, originally called for two small whole chickens, which were trussed and braised on top of the stove. I have substituted chicken pieces because they are easier to serve with rice.

1 tablespoon peeled and minced fresh ginger	1 chicken, 3-4 pounds, cut into pieces
1 tablespoon cardamom	4 teaspoons salt
1 teaspoon fennel seeds	2 whole cloves
½ teaspoon cayenne	1 cinnamon stick
6 tablespoons vegetable oil	2 cups finely chopped onion

In a small bowl, combine the ginger, cardamom, fennel, cayenne and 2 tablespoons of the oil to form a paste.

Rub the chicken pieces with the salt and then coat with the paste. Refrigerate for at least 1 hour or overnight so that the chicken absorbs the flavors.

In a heavy casserole dish or Dutch oven large enough to hold the chicken, heat the remaining 4 tablespoons oil over medium heat. Add the cinnamon stick and cloves and stir until they are evenly coated with oil. Add the onion and continue to cook until golden, about 15 minutes.

Add the chicken to the pot; pour any extra spice paste on top. Cook the chicken over medium-high heat, turning frequently, until lightly browned. Stir in ½ cup water and bring to a boil. Immediately reduce the heat to low. To seal tightly, cover with aluminum foil, securing it around the edges. Place the lid of the casserole on top and continue to cook for 45 minutes, until the chicken is tender but not falling apart. Remove from the heat and let the chicken rest, covered, for 10 to 20 minutes before serving.

Serves 4 to 6.

Chicken with Potatoes

(Maaoude B'tata)

CHICKEN WITH POTATOES is the favorite choice for the Syrian Shabbat meal. This recipe came from Hugette Galante, a gifted cook from Syria. A variation substitutes eggplant for the potatoes. If you are using eggplant, cut it into cubes, salt them and let them stand for 20 minutes, then squeeze out the excess liquid before frying.

1 4-pound chicken	Salt and pepper
2 tablespoons vegetable oil, plus 1- 2 cups for frying	1 cup water
8-10 russet potatoes, peeled and cubed	Juice from 1 lemon

Wash the chicken well. Heat the 2 tablespoons oil in a large pot over medium-low heat. Put the chicken in the pot, cover and cook for 30 minutes, turning occasionally. Reduce the heat to low and continue cooking for 15 to 30 minutes more, until the chicken is dry and the meat falls easily from the bones. Turn off the heat and let cool. Preheat the oven to 350°F.

Heat the 1 to 2 cups oil in a deep pot to 350°F; a cube of bread tossed in will brown quickly. Add the potato cubes and fry in batches until golden, turning to brown on all sides. Remove them with a slotted spoon and allow the potatoes to drain on paper towels.

Remove the skin and bones from the chicken. Break the chicken up into pieces.

Place the potatoes and the chicken in a baking dish. Sprinkle with salt and pepper. Add the water and lemon juice. Cover with aluminum foil and bake for 30 minutes to blend the flavors. Serve on a large platter.

Serves 6.

Chicken Oregano

HIS SIMPLE MARINATED CHICKEN can be grilled or roasted. Try it with garlicky *azada* sauce (page 254) on the side. The recipe was given to me by a woman named Sophia who moved to Los Angeles from Athens after World War II. Her family originally came from Salonika, which had been a thriving Jewish community before the war.

½ cup extra-virgin olive oil	1 teaspoon salt, or to taste
¼ cup lemon juice	½ teaspoon pepper
2 garlic cloves, finely chopped	1 3-pound chicken, cut into
1 tablespoon crushed dried oregano (fresh can also be used)	serving pieces

In a large bowl, combine the oil, lemon juice and garlic and whisk until smooth and creamy. Stir in the oregano, salt and pepper. Add the chicken pieces and turn them several times so that they are coated on all sides with the marinade.

Arrange the chicken pieces in a single layer in a large baking pan. Pour the remaining marinade mixture over the chicken. Cover and set aside in the refrigerator to marinate for at least 3 hours or overnight.

If you plan to roast the chicken, preheat the oven to 350°F. Roast for 18 to 20 minutes per pound, about 1 hour. To grill the chicken, preheat the grill. Grill the chicken over glowing coals about 4 inches from the heat, turning the pieces occasionally, until the meat shows no traces of pink, about 15 minutes. Serve with Garlic Sauce.

Serves 4 to 6.

INDIA
Chicken in Lemon Sauce
(Mukmuka)

GENERALLY COOK THIS STEWED CHICKEN with a sweet-and-sour broth on Thursday and refrigerate it overnight in a reheatable casserole dish so that the flavors are absorbed into the bird. The next day, I skim off the surface fat, reheat it on the stove and serve it with white rice.

The recipe comes from a Calcuttan woman whom I met in a study group in Los Angeles. Like most Jewish families in Calcutta, hers had come originally from Iraq. She was familiar with all the Iraqi dishes that I prepared, yet her food was distinctly Indian in flavor.

2	tablespoons vegetable oil	1	teaspoon pepper, or to taste
1	large onion, chopped	1	4-pound chicken, cut into
1	garlic clove, minced		serving pieces
1	teaspoon peeled and minced	2	tablespoons dark raisins
	fresh ginger	1¼	cups water
½	teaspoon turmeric	¼	cup lemon juice
1	teaspoon salt, or to taste	1	teaspoon sugar

In a large skillet, heat the oil over medium-high heat. Add the onion, garlic, ginger, turmeric, salt and pepper. Sauté for 3 to 5 minutes, until the onion is soft. Add the chicken and cook for about 5 minutes, turning the pieces to brown on all sides. Add the raisins and water. Bring to a boil, reduce the heat to low and simmer for 30 minutes, stirring occasionally. Add the lemon juice and sugar. Continue cooking for 15 minutes to blend the flavors, then serve.

Serves 4 to 6.

INDIA
Chicken Curry Stew

THIS INDIAN DISH CAPTURES ALL THE FLAVORS OF A TYPICAL CURRY while maintaining the dietary laws of Kashrut. Serve it over rice.

¼ cup vegetable oil
2 large onions, finely chopped
2 garlic cloves, minced
2 teaspoons peeled and minced fresh ginger
2 teaspoons salt
2 teaspoons turmeric
2 teaspoons cumin
1 teaspoon cinnamon

¼ teaspoon cayenne pepper
2 3-pound chickens, cut into serving pieces
2 cups chicken broth, heated
½ cup dark raisins
½ cup slivered, blanched almonds
¼ cup chopped fresh cilantro
Juice from 1 lemon
Chopped fresh parsley for garnish

In a heavy pot large enough to hold the chicken, heat the oil over medium-high heat. Sauté the onion and garlic until golden, about 5 minutes. Add the ginger, salt, turmeric, cumin, cinnamon and cayenne. Add the chicken and brown on all sides, in batches if necessary, about 15 minutes.

Add the chicken broth, raisins, ¼ cup of the almonds and the cilantro. Reduce the heat to low. Cover and simmer, stirring occasionally, for 45 minutes, or until the chicken is tender. Before serving, sprinkle with lemon juice, parsley and the remaining ¼ cup almonds.

Serves 8.

MOROCCO
Chicken with Almonds and Prunes

AT ROSH HASHANAH, the New Year, we serve sweet dishes flavored with honey and dried fruits to remind us of hope and promise. This festive tagine is perfect for that occasion. Like all tagines, it has the consistency of a stew, and it should be served over couscous or white rice.

½	cup blanched almonds	1	tablespoon cinnamon
¼	cup sesame seeds	½	teaspoon turmeric
¼	cup vegetable oil	½	teaspoon salt
2	medium onions, sliced	½	teaspoon pepper
1	4-pound chicken, cut into 8 serving pieces	1	cup water
		3	tablespoons honey
1	cup pitted dried prunes		

Toast the almonds and sesame seeds in a small dry skillet over medium-high heat, stirring constantly, for about 3 minutes, or until light golden. Set aside.

In a large heavy pot, heat the oil over medium-high heat. Add the onion slices and sauté until golden, 5 to 10 minutes. Add the chicken pieces and sauté until golden, about 15 minutes. Add the prunes, cinnamon, turmeric, salt and pepper. Stir in the water, bring to a boil, cover and reduce the heat to low. Simmer for 40 minutes, stirring occasionally.

Before serving, drizzle the honey over the chicken and sprinkle the almonds and sesame seeds on top.

Serves 4 to 6.

ALGERIA
Chicken with Quince

ALTHOUGH IT IS NOT A VERY POPULAR FRUIT in the United States, quince is common in the Maghreb, the western regions of North Africa. The fruit itself resembles an apple but is hard and acidic. You should be able to find quince in a well-stocked produce market in the United States from September through November. Serve this dish over white rice or couscous.

2	tablespoons vegetable oil	¼	cup all-purpose flour
2	pounds onions, thinly sliced	2	medium-large quince, cubed
6	whole chicken legs without skin, about 3½ pounds (2 pounds of cubed lamb may be substituted for chicken; increase cooking time by 30 minutes)	1	teaspoon salt
		½	teaspoon pepper
		½	teaspoon cinnamon
			Pinch of sugar (optional)

In a deep skillet or Dutch oven, heat the oil, add the onion and sauté over medium-high heat until soft, about 4 minutes. Remove and set aside.

Dredge the chicken in the flour and fry in batches for 2 to 3 minutes on each side to brown. Add the onion, quince, salt, pepper, cinnamon and sugar, if using. Add enough water to cover the chicken, about 1½ cups. Bring to a boil, cover, reduce the heat to low and simmer for 1 hour, stirring occasionally to prevent burning. Serve hot.

Serves 4 to 6.

IRAN
Chicken in Walnut and Pomegranate Sauce
(Fesenjan)

PON HEARING THAT I WAS ASSEMBLING RECIPES from her culture, the mother of my children's babysitter, an Iranian woman, sent plates of food for me to sample, including this dish. Although bones and skin add flavor to the stew, the dish can also be made with boneless thigh meat when you're having company. Serve with white basmati rice.

2½	cups walnuts, finely ground	¼	cup tomato paste
¼	cup vegetable oil	¼	cup lemon juice
2	medium onions, finely chopped	¼	cup sugar
2	2-pound chickens, cut into small serving pieces	2	teaspoons salt
		1	teaspoon cinnamon
¼	cup pomegranate syrup (found in Middle Eastern shops)	½	teaspoon pepper
		2½	cups water

In a small dry skillet over medium heat, toast the ground walnuts for 1 to 2 minutes, stirring constantly. Remove them to a medium bowl and set aside.

Heat the oil in a large Dutch oven, add the onion and cook over medium-high heat until soft, about 5 minutes. Remove with a slotted spoon and mix with the walnuts.

Add the chicken to the Dutch oven. Brown all sides and cook for about 10 minutes. Add the walnut-onion mixture plus all remaining ingredients and bring to a boil. Reduce the heat to low and simmer for 1 hour, stirring occasionally to prevent the bottom from burning. Serve hot.

Serves 8.

INDIA
Chicken and Chickpea Stew
(Meetha)

A MEETHA, OR SWEET-AND-SOUR STEW, can be prepared with various ingredients, such as lamb with pumpkin, or chicken with carrots or other vegetables. Lemon juice and brown sugar are added for a delicate sweet-and-sour flavor. The following recipe incorporates chicken with chickpeas. Serve the stew with white rice or pilaf.

2	tablespoons vegetable oil	1	cup water
1	medium onion, sliced	4	cardamom pods
2	garlic cloves, crushed	2	bay leaves
1	teaspoon turmeric	1	15-ounce can chickpeas
1	teaspoon minced fresh ginger		(garbanzo beans), drained
1	teaspoon salt	¼	cup lemon juice
¼	teaspoon pepper	2	tablespoons brown sugar
1	3-pound chicken, cut into 8 serving pieces		

In a Dutch oven, heat the oil over medium-high heat. Add the onion, garlic, turmeric, ginger, salt and pepper. Sauté for 3 minutes, or until the onion is softened.

Add the chicken pieces and sauté for 10 minutes, turning to brown on all sides. Add the water, cardamom pods and bay leaves. Cover and cook for 20 minutes over medium heat, stirring occasionally. Add the chickpeas, lemon juice and brown sugar. Continue cooking for 15 minutes, or until the chicken is fully cooked and the liquid has been reduced to a sauce. Serve hot.

Serves 4 to 6.

Beef and Lamb

Recipes

Lamb Tagine with Raisins and Onions

THE TAGINE, A DISH PARTICULAR TO NORTH AFRICA, is a wonderfully spiced, aromatic stew slowly cooked to rich perfection. Its name comes from the pot in which it is cooked: a tagine, which is a half-glazed earthen pot with a conical lid. A tagine pot can be simple, or it can be intricate and beautifully crafted. In my kitchen, a heavy pot with a tight-fitting lid does the job, although a tagine pot is on my wish list. The most popular tagines are made with lamb, but they can also be prepared with chicken, beef or fish. The ingredients can vary from salted lemons and olives to prunes, onions and almonds, and the dish is always served with rice or couscous. This version is one of my favorite dishes to serve at Rosh Hashanah, when sweet flavors are appropriate. It tastes even better the day after it is made.

½	cup vegetable oil	1	teaspoon cinnamon
4	pounds small onions, peeled and left whole	1	teaspoon salt
4	pounds lamb shoulder, cut into 2-inch pieces	1	teaspoon turmeric or saffron threads
½	pound dark raisins		About 3 cups chicken broth or water

Heat the oil in a Dutch oven over medium-high heat. Add the onions and sauté for 5 minutes, until browned on all sides. Add the meat and sauté in batches to brown, about 10 to 20 minutes total. Add the raisins, cinnamon, salt and turmeric or saffron.

Add enough chicken broth or water to almost cover the meat, reduce the heat to low and simmer for about 2 hours, or until the meat is fully cooked and falls apart easily. Serve hot.

Serves 6.

TUNISIA

Lamb with Artichokes

I WAS INTRODUCED TO THIS TAGINE during a Passover meal served by my friend Nicole Halfon. The combination of artichoke hearts, potatoes and lamb with the strong lemon flavoring is sensuous, and the stew takes on a bright yellow tinge from the turmeric. The preparation of the lemons is a bit unusual. They are peeled of their yellow rind, leaving the white pith, and are then quartered and cooked in the stew. The method imparts a tangy lemon flavor that is subtler than zest or dried lemons and stronger than mere lemon juice.

¼ cup vegetable oil

3 onions, chopped

2 pounds lamb neck, cut into pieces

1 pound lamb shanks with
   bones, cut into pieces

1 teaspoon turmeric
   Salt and pepper to taste

2 lemons, cut into quarters with
   the outer yellow rind removed

3 garlic cloves, chopped
   About 3 cups water

5 boiling potatoes, peeled and quartered

15 fresh artichoke hearts, or 1
   3-pound box frozen

Heat the oil in a Dutch oven over medium-high heat. Add the onions, lamb, turmeric and salt and pepper. Cook over medium heat for 20 minutes.

Add the lemons, garlic and enough water to cover halfway. Cover and simmer for 30 minutes. Add the potatoes and continue cooking for 30 minutes more, stirring occasionally to avoid burning, adding more water if needed. Add the artichoke hearts and continue simmering for 30 minutes more, or until the meat is so tender that it falls off the bones. Remove and discard any bones without meat and serve the tagine hot.

Serves 6.

IRAN
Green Vegetable Stew with Beef
(Qormeh Sabzi)

THIS WONDERFUL IRANIAN STEW IS ONE OF MY FAVORITES. The tart taste of the dried limes simmered with the combination of greens, meat and beans is divine. My first impression of the dish was that it must have spinach as a main ingredient because of its dark green color. In fact, lots and lots of finely chopped parsley gives the stew its notable color. Dried fenugreek adds another complex dimension to the dish.

4	tablespoons vegetable oil	1	bunch leeks or 3 bunches scallions, finely chopped (about 3 cups)
2	medium onions, chopped		
1	pound beef, cut into 1-inch cubes	2	tablespoons dried fenugreek
¼	teaspoon pepper	2-4	whole dried limes (found in Middle Eastern markets)
¼	teaspoon turmeric		
1½	cups water	1	cup canned kidney beans, drained
6	cups finely chopped fresh parsley	1	teaspoon salt

Heat 3 tablespoons of the oil in a Dutch oven over medium-high heat. Add the onions and sauté until browned, about 5 minutes. Add the meat and brown in batches on all sides, about 5 minutes per batch. Add the pepper and turmeric. Add the water and bring to a boil. Reduce the heat to low, cover and simmer for 1 hour, stirring occasionally and adding more water as needed to keep the meat from burning.

Meanwhile, sauté the parsley, leeks or scallions and fenugreek in the remaining 1 tablespoon oil for 5 to 10 minutes, or until wilted. Remove from the heat.

When the meat is almost done, add the sautéed vegetables and the dried limes. Cover and simmer for 1 hour more, or until the meat is fully cooked and is easy to break apart with a fork. As the dried limes cook, poke them several times with a fork to allow the liquid of the stew to enter. About 10 minutes before the stew is done, add the kidney beans and salt. Serve the stew with white rice.

Serves 4 to 6.

Iran

Chopped Lamb Kebabs

(Shefta)

KEBABS ARE SKEWERED PIECES OF MEAT OR CHICKEN roasted over hot coals. Sometimes the meat is finely ground, as in the following recipe, while at other times, pieces of meat are marinated for days in a combination dictated by the family's secret recipe. In my experience, the special ingredient always seems to have something to do with the amount of lemon juice used or with a pinch of sumac, which gives a tart flavor. Serve the kebabs with rice or salads or wrapped in a large piece of flatbread.

1½ pounds lamb, preferably shoulder, twice ground (lean ground beef can be substituted)	1 teaspoon salt
	¼ teaspoon ground sumac (found in Middle Eastern shops)
1 small onion, finely grated, with juices	¼ teaspoon pepper
2 tablespoons finely chopped fresh parsley	Dash of cinnamon and/or allspice
1 teaspoon lemon juice	1 slice good-quality crustless white bread, soaked in water

In a large bowl, mix together the lamb, onion, parsley, lemon juice, salt, sumac, pepper and cinnamon or allspice. Squeeze the excess liquid out of the bread and mix it into the meat mixture. Cover and refrigerate for at least 1 hour or overnight.

Divide the meat mixture into 8 parts and shape each into a cylinder around a metal skewer. Preheat the grill or broiler, with a rack about 5 inches from the heat. Grill or broil the kebabs, turning the skewers so that both sides become browned, about 3 minutes on each side for medium well done, or until the meat is cooked to taste. Serve immediately.

Serves 4.

IRAN
Lamb and Eggplant Casserole

HIS TOMATO AND EGGPLANT CASSEROLE is richly flavored with lamb and has an accent of cinnamon. Salting the eggplant first draws out the bitter juices and prevents it from absorbing so much oil that it becomes greasy.

3 medium eggplants, peeled and sliced in ½-inch rounds	1 large onion, chopped (about 2 cups)
Salt	1 teaspoon turmeric
1 pound ground lamb	1 teaspoon salt
3 tablespoons vegetable oil, plus about ½ cup more for frying	4 large tomatoes, sliced
	2 tablespoons tomato paste, dissolved in ½ cup water
1 teaspoon cinnamon	1 teaspoon sugar

Sprinkle each eggplant slice on both sides with salt. Let the eggplant slices sit in a colander for 20 minutes to drain. Squeeze out the excess moisture, rinse and pat dry.

In a large Dutch oven, brown the meat in the 3 tablespoons oil over medium-high heat. Sprinkle with the cinnamon. Add the onion and continue cooking until soft. Add the turmeric and salt, reduce the heat to low and cook, stirring occasionally, for 15 minutes more, or until the meat is cooked through.

Using the remaining ½ cup oil, brown the eggplant slices in a large skillet. Remove with a slotted spoon and set aside to drain on paper towels. Brown the tomato slices in the same pan and set aside.

Preheat the oven to 350°F.

Place a layer of half the fried eggplant in an ovenproof casserole dish. Cover the eggplant with the meat. Put the tomatoes on top of the meat, followed by the remaining eggplant slices.

In a small bowl, combine the tomato paste mixture and the sugar. Pour the mixture over the casserole. Cover with foil or a lid and bake for 15 to 20 minutes, until bubbling. Serve hot.

Serves 6.

SYRIA

Skewered Lamb or Beef

(Shishlik)

IN THE PUBLIC PARKS ON THE WEEKENDS IN ISRAEL, large gatherings of families enjoy outdoor lunches, and the smell of grilled meat permeates the air. More commonly known as shish kebab here in America, *shishlik* is marinated, skewered meat and vegetables grilled over a charcoal barbecue. Turkey can be substituted for the beef or lamb.

Marinade

3 tablespoons extra-virgin olive oil

Juice from 1 lemon

1 onion, finely grated, with juices

1 teaspoon dried thyme

¾ teaspoon salt

½ teaspoon pepper

½ teaspoon dried oregano

¼ teaspoon sumac or ground dried limes (found in Middle Eastern shops)

2 pounds lamb or beef, cut into 1-inch cubes

1 large eggplant

1 large onion, quartered

10 cherry tomatoes

1 large green pepper, seeded and quartered

Bay leaves

Salt and pepper to taste

To make the marinade: Mix together all the ingredients.

Place the meat in a large bowl, cover with the marinade and turn several times to make sure that all sides are covered. Place in the refrigerator and let marinate for 4 to 5 hours.

Cut the eggplant into ½-inch-thick slices, then quarter each slice. Preheat the grill or broiler, with a rack about 5 inches from the heat. Alternate the meat, onion, tomatoes, green pepper, eggplant and bay leaves on metal skewers. Grill or broil for 4 minutes on each side for medium-rare. Season with salt and pepper and serve immediately.

Serves 4.

EGYPT
Lamb Stew with Mushrooms

THIS MODERN ADAPTATION OF THE TRADITIONAL LAMB STEW was given to me by an Egyptian friend who now lives in America. Tomatoes, green peppers and cilantro give the stew a distinctly Sephardic flavor. Serve with rice.

6 tablespoons olive oil	1 cup small mushrooms, left whole or sliced
1½ pounds lamb, cut into 1-inch cubes	Juice from 1 lemon
2 medium onions, chopped	½ cup chopped fresh cilantro
2 garlic cloves, minced	1 teaspoon salt
4 medium tomatoes, chopped	1 teaspoon pepper
1 large green pepper, chopped	
3 cups chicken broth or water	

Heat 4 tablespoons of the olive oil in a Dutch oven over medium-high heat. Add the lamb in batches and sauté for about 5 minutes, turning to brown all sides. Remove the lamb with a slotted spoon and set aside. Add the onion and garlic and sauté until golden, about 5 minutes. Add the tomatoes and green pepper and cook for 5 minutes, then add the lamb and the broth or water.

Cover, reduce the heat to low and simmer for 1½ hours. In a small skillet, sauté the mushrooms in the remaining 2 tablespoons olive oil and add them to the pot along with the lemon juice, cilantro, salt and pepper. Simmer for 30 minutes more, stirring occasionally. Serve hot.

Serves 4.

ALGERIA

Beef Stew with Turnips
(D'fina)

N THE MIDDLE EAST, turnips often appear pickled, braised, boiled or cooked in stews, as in the following recipe. This simple stew from Algeria is served for Shabbat lunch, accompanied by marinated salads.

3 tablespoons vegetable oil	1 teaspoon turmeric
2 medium onions, coarsely chopped	Cayenne pepper
2 pounds London broil, cut into 2-inch pieces	8 cups water
3 small white turnips, peeled and cubed	**Roasted Brown Eggs** (optional)
1½ teaspoons salt	6 raw large eggs in their shells

In a heavy lidded pot or Dutch oven, heat the oil over medium-high heat. Add the onion and sauté for 5 minutes, or until soft. Add the meat and sauté on all sides for about 10 minutes to brown. Add the turnips and cook for 10 minutes.

Add the salt, turmeric and cayenne to taste. Add the water and bring to a boil, then reduce the heat to low.

Add the eggs, if using, to the pot and simmer the stew, covered, over low heat for 2 hours, or transfer to a crockpot, cook at the lowest setting overnight and serve the next day for lunch.

Serves 6.

MOROCCO
Shabbat Stew
(Scheena)

DISHES KNOWN AS SCHEENA are variations of a one-dish meal that is cooked slowly over a low flame, a flame that must be lit before Shabbat begins. The sentimental attachment to these traditional dishes cannot be overestimated.

In Morocco, this stew was prepared in earthenware casseroles that were tightly sealed and slowly cooked in the public baker's oven from Friday before Shabbat until Saturday afternoon, when it was served. Now we use electric crockpots or an oven set at low.

2	cups raw long-grain white rice	1	whole garlic head, unpeeled
3	tablespoons vegetable oil	6-8	raw eggs (1 per person) in their shells
4	pounds short ribs or other fatty meat	4	medium boiling potatoes, peeled and halved
1	medium onion, halved	4	medium sweet potatoes, peeled and halved
1	cup cooked chickpeas (garbanzo beans), prepared from ½ cup dried	2	teaspoons salt
4	dates	1	teaspoon pepper

If you are planning to cook the dish in the oven, preheat the oven to 200°F. In a small skillet, sauté the rice for about 3 minutes in 1 tablespoon of the oil, stirring constantly. Wrap the rice loosely in cheesecloth and set aside.

In a large skillet, sauté the meat and onion in the remaining 2 tablespoons oil for 10 minutes, or until browned.

Put the chickpeas and dates in a deep lidded pot or Dutch oven or crockpot. Place the meat and garlic head on top. Put the rice (in its cheesecloth) on top of the meat. Arrange the eggs in their shells on top of the rice. Top with both kinds of potatoes. Add the salt and pepper and enough water to cover all the ingredients. Bring to a boil, simmer for 15 minutes, cover and remove from the stove. Place the pot on the top rack of the oven or set the crockpot at low and cook for 6 hours or overnight.

To serve, separate the contents, placing the eggs in one dish, the rice in another and the potatoes and meat in another.

Serves 6 to 8.

VARIATION

Meat Loaf Cooked in Scheena

If you have a bit more time, adding a meat loaf gives extra flavor and aroma for an especially rich and festive *scheena*.

1	pound ground beef or turkey	1	teaspoon mace
¼	pound walnuts, coarsely chopped	1	teaspoon sugar
¼	cup vegetable oil	1	teaspoon salt
2	large eggs	1	teaspoon pepper
6	tablespoons bread crumbs	¼	teaspoon ginger
1	teaspoon cinnamon	¼	teaspoon nutmeg

Combine all the ingredients in a large bowl and mix thoroughly. Wrap the mixture loosely in cheesecloth. Place the meat loaf under the potatoes in the *scheena* and cook as directed. To serve, remove the meat loaf, discard the cheesecloth, slice and serve in a separate dish.

TUNISIA

Beef Stew with Spinach, Mint and White Beans

(T'fina B'kaila)

T'FINAS, SLOW-COOKING STEWS, are beloved by Tunisian Jews, who give them the nickname Queen. This dish is known as the Black Queen, since it turns almost black from the charred spinach.

4 pounds (about 6 10-ounce bags) fresh spinach, stems removed	1 teaspoon dried rose petals (optional)
½ cup vegetable oil	1 cinnamon stick
8 ounces small white dried beans	1½ teaspoons salt
1 medium onion, finely chopped	1 teaspoon pepper
6 garlic cloves, put through a garlic press	8 cups water
10 fresh mint leaves, finely chopped	2 pounds beef, cut into 2-inch cubes
2 teaspoons coriander	

Wash the spinach and pat dry. Fry it in batches in the oil on high heat until all the liquid has evaporated and the spinach is dark, almost charred but not burned. Remove from the heat immediately and transfer to a bowl. Mash the spinach with a wooden spoon until it becomes a paste.

Place all the ingredients except the meat in a large heavy pot with a lid and bring to a boil. Add the meat, cover, reduce the heat to medium and cook for 30 minutes. Reduce the heat to low and simmer for 2 hours, stirring occasionally. Or transfer to a crockpot and cook at the lowest setting overnight. The longer this dish cooks, the better it tastes.

Serves 6.

TUNISIA
Spicy Beef Stew with White Beans
(T'fina Camounia)

T HE SLOW COOKING and the addition of hot pepper sauce give this stew a reddish brown color, which accounts for its name, "the Red Queen." The flavors in the dish are rich and spicy, with lots of garlic and cumin.

8	cups water	5	boiling potatoes, halved (optional)
8	ounces small white dried beans	10	garlic cloves, crushed
½	cup vegetable oil	2	teaspoons cumin
2	pounds beef (London broil or other stewing meat), cut into 2-to-3-inch cubes	1½	teaspoons salt
		1	teaspoon paprika
4	large eggs in their shells	1	teaspoon *harissa* (hot pepper sauce)
			Lemon slices for garnish

In a large lidded pot or Dutch oven, bring the water to a boil. Add the beans and oil and bring to a boil again. Add the meat and eggs in their shells. Cover, reduce the heat to low and simmer for 2 hours. Add the potatoes (if using), garlic and spices. If you are preparing this dish for Shabbat lunch, add 2 more cups water, cover, reduce the heat to the lowest setting and continue to cook overnight. Otherwise, uncover and cook for 1 hour more, or until the beans are tender and the potatoes are cooked through.

To serve, remove the eggs from the pot, peel them and cut them in half. Spoon portions of the stew into dishes. Top with the lemon slices and egg halves. Season with more *harissa*, if desired.

Serves 6.

EGYPT

Braised Meat Loaf with Cumin
(Belehat)

BELEHAT, A MEAT LOAF WITH HARD-BOILED EGGS IN THE CENTER, can be served hot or cold. The sliced meat loaf on a platter is a very attractive dish.

2	pounds ground beef (turkey can be substituted)	2	hard-boiled eggs, shelled
1	tablespoon all-purpose flour	2	large eggs, beaten
3-4	garlic cloves, minced		Bread crumbs
1	teaspoon cumin	½	cup vegetable oil
1	teaspoon salt	1	cup water
½	teaspoon pepper	1	cup tomato sauce
	Pinch of allspice	1	bay leaf or sprig of thyme

Place the ground meat on a work surface sprinkled with the flour. Knead in the garlic and spices and spread out the meat. Place the hard-boiled eggs on top and roll the meat around them to form a loaf. Brush the loaf with the beaten eggs and then roll the loaf in bread crumbs.

Heat the oil in a Dutch oven and brown the loaf, turning it so that all sides are browned. Add the water, tomato sauce and bay leaf or thyme. Cover, reduce the heat to low and cook for 30 minutes. Serve hot or cold.

Serves 4.

SYRIA

Squash Stuffed with Rice and Meat
(Mersche)

THE GREEN SQUASHES traditionally used for this dish are pale green and rather short and fat in comparison to the dark green zucchini available in American markets, but zucchini are a fine substitute. This recipe came from my friend Danielle Zagha, who is active in the Sephardic community in Los Angeles. She carries on the traditions of generosity and service by preparing Sephardic food with mastery.

Meat and Rice Filling

½ pound lean ground lamb, beef or turkey

⅓ cup raw long-grain white rice, washed

1-2 teaspoons olive oil

1 teaspoon allspice

½ teaspoon cinnamon

½ teaspoon salt, or to taste

⅓ cup water

8 medium green koosa squashes or zucchini, left whole, stem end removed, hollowed out with an apple corer

Sauce

2 tablespoons pomegranate syrup (found in Middle Eastern specialty shops)

1 tablespoon tomato paste

Juice from 1 lemon

8 dried apricots, cut into pieces

1 tablespoon sugar

½ teaspoon salt

2 cups water

To make the filling: Mix all the ingredients together.

Fill the squashes loosely with the meat and rice mixture. Preheat the oven to 350°F.

To make the sauce: In a small saucepan, combine all the ingredients and bring to a boil, stirring occasionally. Remove from the heat.

Place the squashes in a heavy pot or a Dutch oven. Add a little water, cover and steam for 15 minutes.

Pour the sauce over the squashes. Cover and bake until they are tender and the filling is cooked through, about 40 minutes, and serve.

Serves 4 as a main dish, 8 as a side dish.

MOROCCO

Moroccan Hamburgers

(Kefta)

KEFTA, A SMALL HAMBURGER, is a popular side dish that blends ground meat with a variety of herbs and sometimes vegetables. I serve it as a main course with rice and salad. It tastes best when all the preparations have been made a few hours before cooking, allowing the meat to absorb the flavors of the seasonings.

2 pounds ground beef, lamb or turkey	1 teaspoon cumin
¼ cup chopped fresh parsley	Salt and pepper
¼ cup chopped fresh cilantro	½ teaspoon cayenne pepper (optional)
8 garlic cloves, minced	¼ cup vegetable oil
2 teaspoons paprika	¼ cup water or lemon juice

In a medium bowl, mix the meat, parsley, cilantro and garlic. Add the paprika, cumin and salt and pepper to taste, then mix in the oil and water or lemon juice. Form the meat into small hamburgers and broil, barbecue or panfry. Serve hot.

Makes 8 to 10 little hamburgers.

MEAT AND POTATO PATTIES

(KTZI ZTOT)

MEAT WAS AN IMPORTANT AND EXPENSIVE INGREDIENT in the Sephardic communities. Creative techniques were devised to stretch small quantities of meat to feed a large family. Traditionally, *ktzi ztots* were served as a side dish among many other dishes for a feast. These little burgers are wonderful as a main course served with rice and salad.

2	boiling potatoes, peeled	1	teaspoon turmeric
2	pounds ground meat (lamb, beef, turkey or chicken)	2	large eggs, lightly beaten
			Salt and pepper to taste
½	cup finely chopped celery		
½	cup finely chopped onion		Vegetable oil for frying
¼	cup finely chopped parsley		

In a large pot, boil the potatoes until soft. Empty the water out of the pot and continue to cook the potatoes a little longer until they are dry. Mash with a masher or fork (do not use a food processor). Let cool.

Combine the meat, celery, onion, parsley, turmeric, eggs and salt and pepper with the cooled potatoes. Knead the mixture together with your hands. Form into patties about 3 to 4 inches in diameter. Pour about ½ inch of oil into a large skillet and fry until golden brown, about 3 minutes on each side. Place on paper towels to drain. Serve immediately.

Makes 10 patties; serves 4 to 6.

SYRIA

Leeks and Meatballs in Sweet-and-Sour Sauce

ONE EXPLANATION FOR THE POPULARITY of sweet-and-sour dishes is that food should not be too sweet lest it attract the evil eye, so a little sour is added. Whatever the origin, I adore the combination.

2 pounds (about 3 large) leeks

Meatballs

1 pound ground beef
1 large egg
¼ cup matzo meal
½ teaspoon salt
   Pinch each of cinnamon
   and allspice
2 tablespoons olive oil

Sauce

1 8-ounce can tomato sauce
½ cup chopped celery
½ cup water
2 tablespoons brown sugar
2 garlic cloves, crushed
½ teaspoon dried mint
2 tablespoons apricot preserves
   Juice from 1 lemon

Wash the leeks well; cut off the roots and the outer layer. Cut the light green parts lengthwise and into 1-inch sections. Set aside in cold water.

To make the meatballs: In a medium bowl, combine the beef, egg, matzo meal, salt, cinnamon and allspice. Form into 1½-inch balls. Heat the oil in a deep pot and brown the meatballs in batches over medium-high heat for about 5 minutes, turning occasionally.

Drain the leeks and add them to the pot with the meatballs; set aside, off the heat.

To make the sauce: In a medium saucepan over medium heat, combine the tomato sauce, celery, water, brown sugar, garlic, mint and preserves and cook for 10 minutes, stirring occasionally.

Pour the sauce over the meatballs and leeks. Cook, covered, over medium heat for 45 minutes, or until the leeks are very tender. Add the lemon juice and serve hot.

Serves 4.

Meatballs with Celery

IT SEEMS AS IF EACH SEPHARDIC CULTURE HAS A MEATBALL RECIPE that is considered the Friday-night special. This dish is a Shabbat favorite in Morocco.

Meatballs

3 pounds ground beef

1 medium onion, finely chopped

½ cup chopped fresh parsley

1 large egg

¼ cup bread crumbs, or 4 slices
good-quality white bread,
soaked and squeezed dry

4 tablespoons olive oil

½ teaspoon mace

½ teaspoon cinnamon

½ teaspoon nutmeg

Salt and pepper to taste

3 tablespoons water

Celery

2 tablespoons vegetable oil

8 garlic cloves, thinly sliced

4 pounds fresh celery, cubed

½ teaspoon turmeric

Juice from 1 lemon

Salt and pepper to taste

To make the meatballs: Mix together the ground beef, onion, parsley, egg, bread crumbs or bread, olive oil, spices, salt, pepper and water. Dampen your hands with water or oil and shape the mixture into balls the size of small apricots. If possible, set aside for 1 hour before cooking to allow the spices to flavor the meat. Cook the meatballs in a large heavy pot in 2 cups boiling water for 30 minutes, or until fully cooked. Set the meatballs aside; reserve the liquid.

To make the celery: In a small skillet, heat the oil over medium heat and briefly sauté the garlic until softened, about 3 minutes. Add the garlic to the reserved meatball liquid, along with the celery and turmeric, and cook over medium heat for 30 minutes. Add the meatballs and lemon juice, and simmer for 15 minutes longer, or until the celery is soft. Season with salt and pepper. Serve hot.

Serves 6 to 8.

Tunisian Meatballs
(Boulettes)

THESE ARE A LOT OF WORK, BUT THEY ARE REALLY GOOD. You can make them ahead of time and freeze them after frying. When you are ready to use them, do not defrost; just steam or cook them in the sauce. Serve the meatballs as a side dish with Tunisian Couscous (page 98).

Meatballs

1-2 medium onions, coarsely chopped
½ cup coarsely chopped fresh parsley
   Salt
8 slices day-old good-quality white bread
1 artichoke heart, thinly sliced
1 medium russet potato, peeled and thinly sliced
1 zucchini, about 6 inches long, sliced into thin rounds
3 garlic cloves, minced
½ teaspoon allspice

1 pound ground beef
1 teaspoon pepper
   All-purpose flour for dredging
3 large eggs

   Vegetable oil for frying

Sauce

1 tablespoon vegetable oil
1 garlic clove, mashed
1 6-ounce can tomato paste
½ cup water

To make the meatballs: Process the chopped onions and parsley in a blender or food processor fitted with the metal blade so that they are minced very fine. Transfer to a strainer and sprinkle with salt. Let stand for 15 minutes, then squeeze out the excess moisture. Set aside.

Soak the bread for 10 minutes in water. Squeeze out the excess water and break the bread into pieces.

Sprinkle salt on the artichoke heart, potato and zucchini and set aside. After 15 minutes, rinse and pat dry with paper towels.

In a medium bowl, combine the onion-parsley mixture, bread, garlic and allspice. Mix in the beef. Shape the mixture into small balls about the size of walnuts and press 1 or 2 slices of vegetables onto the side of each meatball; the vegetables will stick.

Spread flour onto a large plate. In a small bowl, beat the eggs with a pinch of salt.

Pour about 3 inches of oil into a deep pot and heat to 350°F; a cube of bread tossed in will brown quickly.

Roll the meatballs in the flour and then dip them into the eggs. Add the meatballs to the oil a few at a time and fry until brown, about 3 to 5 minutes. Drain on paper towels.

To make the sauce: In a separate large pot, heat the oil over medium heat, add the garlic and cook until lightly colored, about 1 to 2 minutes. Combine the tomato paste and water in a small bowl and add to the pot. Add the meatballs to the pot. Reduce the heat to low, cover and simmer for 45 minutes. Serve warm.

Serves 4 to 6.

IRAQ
MEAT-FILLED POTATO PANCAKES
(POTATO KUBBEH)

MY MOTHER-IN-LAW USED TO MAKE these wonderful little stuffed potato pancakes for Friday evening. The potatoes are boiled, then grated. Do not mash them or grind them in a food processor. If you do, the dough will not hold together well.

5 boiling potatoes, peeled	1 teaspoon pepper
2 tablespoons olive oil	1 large egg, lightly beaten
½ medium onion, finely chopped	2 tablespoons all-purpose flour
½ pound ground beef, lamb or turkey	
A few celery leaves, finely chopped	Vegetable oil for frying
1 teaspoon salt	

Boil the potatoes in salted water until fully cooked but firm; they should not be mushy. Pour off the water and cook for a few seconds over medium heat to remove the moisture from the potatoes. Set aside to cool.

Heat the olive oil in a skillet over medium-high heat. Sauté the onion and meat until the onion is golden, about 5 minutes. Add the celery leaves and salt and pepper to taste. Set aside to cool.

Grate the cooked potatoes on the medium-sized holes of a hand-held grater. Add the salt and pepper. Gently mix in the egg. Sprinkle in the flour, 1 tablespoon at a time, kneading well to make a pliable dough.

Divide the potato dough into 12 portions and shape into balls. Flatten each potato ball into a patty with the palm of your hand. Put 1 tablespoon of the meat mixture in the center of each patty and bring the edges of the dough up, pinching together to cover the filling. The *kubbeh* should be about 2 inches in diameter, like a stuffed pancake.

Pour about ½ inch of oil into a skillet over medium-high heat. Add the patties a few at a time and fry, turning once, until golden on both sides, about 3 minutes per side.

Drain on paper towels. Serve warm or at room temperature.

Makes 12 kubbeh; serves 4 to 6.

MIDDLE EAST

Vegetables Stuffed with Rice, Ground Beef and Mint
(Mehashi)

EVERY SEPHARDIC CULTURE has stuffed-vegetable dishes that are customarily served for Shabbat and other festive meals. Almost any vegetable can be used: onions, tomatoes, eggplants, green peppers, zucchini, even carrots and cucumbers. Most of the cooks I know make an assortment of stuffed vegetables in the same pot so that the flavors blend while the vegetables cook.

6-8 medium onions, tomatoes, green peppers or zucchini

Stuffing

2 tablespoons olive oil
1 medium onion, chopped
2 garlic cloves, minced
1½ cups raw long-grain white rice
2 tablespoons water
1 pound ground beef, lamb or turkey
¼ cup finely chopped fresh mint leaves

Salt and pepper
Juice from 1 lemon, or 1 tablespoon white vinegar
1 tablespoon tomato paste

Sauce

½ 6-ounce can tomato paste
Juice from 1 lemon
2 tablespoons olive oil
1 tablespoon sugar
1½ cups water

To prepare the vegetables for stuffing: To prepare onions, remove the paperlike outer skin, then immerse the whole onions in boiling water for 2 minutes. Remove with a slotted spoon and let cool. Make a vertical slit halfway into each onion and peel off the layers to create a cavity for the stuffing. To prepare tomatoes, cut off the tops and hollow out the centers to create shells. To prepare peppers, cut off the stem ends and scoop out the seeds. To prepare zucchini, cut off the stem ends and hollow the vegetables out with an apple corer.

To make the stuffing: Heat the oil in a medium skillet and sauté the onion and garlic over medium-high heat until golden, about 4 minutes. Add the rice and water and sauté for 4 minutes. Remove from the heat.

Combine the rice mixture with the meat, mint, salt and pepper to taste, lemon juice or vinegar and tomato paste. Mix well and set aside.

To make the sauce: Combine all the ingredients in a small bowl.

Loosely fill the vegetables with the stuffing mixture. Place them tightly side by side in a pot just large enough to hold them snugly. Pour in the sauce and bring to a boil. Reduce the heat to low, cover and continue cooking for 45 minutes, adding water if necessary to prevent the vegetable bottoms from burning, until the vegetables are soft and the filling is cooked through. Serve hot or warm.

Serves 4 to 6.

YEMEN

Yemenite Vegetables Stuffed with Lamb and Rice

THE FILLING USED IN THIS RECIPE, a combination of lamb and rice that is accented with dill and mint, can also be used to stuff grape leaves.

4-6 medium green peppers, tomatoes, eggplants or zucchini	½ teaspoon dried mint Salt and pepper to taste

Stuffing	**Sauce**
½ pound ground lamb	¾ cup water
1 medium onion, finely chopped	¼ cup olive oil
½ cup raw long-grain white rice	Juice from 1 lemon
2 tablespoons chopped tomato	1 teaspoon sugar
½ teaspoon dried dill	

To prepare the vegetables for stuffing, follow the directions on page 167.

To make the stuffing: Brown the meat in a skillet over medium-high heat, breaking up the pieces as it cooks. Remove with a slotted spoon and set aside. Add the onion and sauté for several minutes. Add the rice, tomato, dill, mint and salt and pepper and cook for 5 minutes. Remove the rice mixture and combine it with the meat. Set aside to cool.

Loosely fill the vegetables with the stuffing mixture. Place them tightly side by side in a pot just large enough to hold them snugly.

To make the sauce: Combine all the ingredients in a small bowl. Pour the sauce over the vegetables. Bring to a boil, reduce the heat to low, cover and continue cooking for 45 minutes, adding water if necessary to prevent the vegetable bottoms from burning, until the vegetables are soft and the filling is cooked through.

Serves 2 to 4.

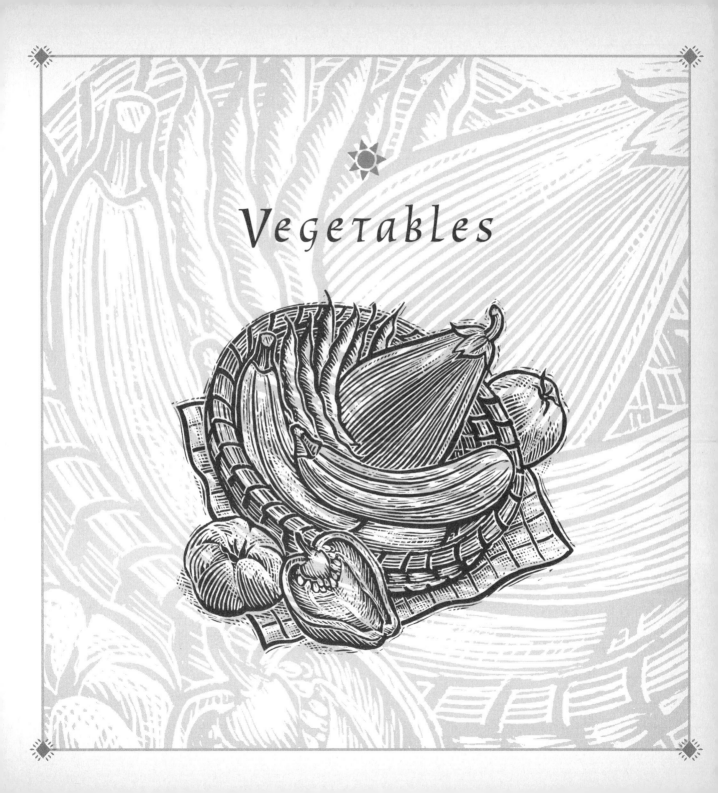

Vegetables

Recipes

GREECE

Tomatoes Stuffed with Cheese

THIS IS A GOOD VEGETARIAN SIDE DISH. The stuffing combines the sharp flavor of feta cheese with the mildness of hoop cheese. If you cannot find hoop cheese, large-curd cottage cheese is a practical substitute. Drain the cottage cheese through a double thickness of cheesecloth and squeeze a little to remove the excess whey and liquids. A good Middle Eastern cook would leave the cheese suspended over a sink or pail for a day, allowing the cheese to dry out, but few of us have the patience to wait that long.

3	pounds large tomatoes	1½	cups grated hoop cheese
	Sugar		or other semisoft white cheese,
	Salt		such as cottage cheese, ricotta
1	cup crumbled feta cheese		or pot cheese
		2	large eggs, lightly beaten

Preheat the oven to 300°F.

Core the tomatoes, cut them in half and scoop out the insides, leaving shells about ¼ inch thick. Sprinkle ½ teaspoon sugar and a little salt into each tomato shell. Mix the cheeses with the eggs. Fill each tomato shell about halfway with the cheese mixture.

Place the tomatoes side by side in a baking dish large enough to hold them snugly. Bake for 15 to 20 minutes, or until the tomatoes are softened and the cheese is cooked. Serve immediately.

Serves 4 to 6.

RHODES

Stuffed Tomatoes and Peppers

(Reyenades)

FOR THIS VEGETARIAN RENDITION OF STUFFED VEGETABLES, other vegetables, such as onions, beets, zucchini and even cucumbers, may be substituted.

6 large, firm tomatoes
6 medium green peppers

Stuffing
2 tablespoons olive oil
1 medium onion, finely chopped
1 large tomato, peeled, seeded and chopped
4 tablespoons pine nuts
¼ cup dried currants
2 tablespoons finely chopped fresh dill

2 tablespoons finely chopped fresh parsley
1 teaspoon dried thyme
   Salt and pepper to taste
2 cups raw long-grain white rice

Sauce
¼ cup olive oil
   Juice from 1 lemon
2 tablespoons sugar

Slice off the tops of the tomatoes and green peppers. Carefully remove the pulp of each tomato, leaving a shell with walls about ¼ inch thick, and set the pulp aside; discard the seeds of the peppers.

To make the stuffing: In a large skillet, heat the olive oil and sauté the onion until transparent, about 4 minutes. Add the reserved tomato pulp, chopped tomato, pine nuts, currants, herbs and salt and pepper. Continue cooking for 2 to 3 minutes to soften the tomato. Add the rice and about 1 inch of water, cover and simmer until the water has been absorbed, about 5 minutes.

Preheat the oven to 350°F.

Fill the tomatoes and peppers with the stuffing and set them tightly side by side in a baking dish just large enough to hold the vegetables snugly. Add enough water so that the liquid reaches halfway up the sides of the tomatoes.

To make the sauce: Combine the olive oil, lemon juice and sugar in a small bowl and pour over the stuffed vegetables.

Cover with aluminum foil and bake for 45 minutes, until the vegetables are soft and the filling is cooked through. To serve, carefully remove the stuffed vegetables from the baking dish, freeing the bottoms from the pan with a spatula, and transfer them to a serving platter.

Serves 6 as a main dish, 12 as a side dish.

IRAQ
Eggplants Stuffed with Chickpeas and Mint

WHEN I ASKED MY MOTHER-IN-LAW why stuffing vegetables is such a popular way to prepare them in Sephardic cooking, she answered that things are not always as they seem on the surface; sometimes the true substance lies beneath. With these vegetables, the stuffing indeed supplies the essence of the dish.

Stuffing
½ cup dried chickpeas (garbanzo beans), soaked overnight
1¼ cups raw long-grain white rice, washed
2 medium tomatoes, chopped
½ cup chopped green onions
½ cup finely chopped fresh parsley
¼ cup chopped fresh mint, or 2 teaspoons dried mint
1 teaspoon salt

¼ teaspoon cinnamon
¼ teaspoon pepper
⅛ teaspoon dried thyme
½ cup olive oil
  Juice from 2 lemons

Eggplants
12 Japanese or small regular eggplants
¼ cup olive oil
4 large tomatoes, sliced
2 garlic cloves, chopped

To make the stuffing: Boil the soaked chickpeas in water to cover for 15 minutes. They should remain firm. Drain. Put the chickpeas in a food processor fitted with the metal blade and coarsely chop, pulsing; do not puree. Transfer to a medium bowl. Add the remaining ingredients and mix well. Set aside.

To prepare the eggplants: Cut off the tops of the eggplants. Using the tip of a potato peeler, hollow out the center of each eggplant. Soak the hollowed-out eggplants in salted water for 10 minutes to take away their bitter taste, then drain and pat dry. Fill the eggplants loosely with the stuffing mixture; it will expand during cooking.

In a skillet large enough to hold the eggplants in a single layer, heat the oil. Arrange half the tomatoes and garlic in the skillet. Place the eggplants on top of the tomatoes and garlic, closely packed together. Top with the remaining tomatoes and garlic.

Add enough water to cover the eggplants. Place an inverted plate on top of the stuffed vegetables; it should cover the pan securely. Bring to a boil, reduce the heat to low and simmer until the liquid has been absorbed and the eggplants are tender, about 20 minutes.

Serves 6 as a main dish, 12 as a side dish.

EGYPT
Fava Beans
(Ful)

AVA BEANS ARE THE OLDEST CULTIVATED BEANS IN EUROPE. *Ful* is a common breakfast dish in Egypt; I serve it as a side dish or as part of a Shabbat brunch. Fava beans, which are also called broad beans, can be purchased fresh, frozen, canned or dried.

About 3 cups fresh fava beans, or 1½ cups dried

6 large hard-boiled eggs, peeled

¾ cup Tahina (page 38)

6 tablespoons olive oil

1-2 small onions, finely chopped

¼ cup finely chopped fresh parsley

If using fresh fava beans, bring a large pot of salted water to a boil and open the bean casings. Pop the beans into the boiling water and cook until tender, about 40 minutes. The outer bean skins will turn from green to brown.

To cook dried beans, soak them overnight in water three times their volume. The next day, drain, rinse, cover with fresh water and bring to a boil in a medium pot. Cover, reduce the heat to low and simmer for 1½ hours. Add 1 teaspoon salt when the beans begin to soften. Drain the beans and use as directed.

Divide the cooked beans among 6 soup plates. Chop each hard-boiled egg and place on top of each portion of beans. On top of the egg, place 1 to 2 tablespoons tahina and 1 tablespoon olive oil. Serve hot, garnished with the chopped onion and parsley. Pita bread makes a nice accompaniment.

Serves 6.

Green Beans in Tomato Sauce

(Fasoulia)

IRECEIVED RECIPES SIMILAR TO THIS ONE from women of Rhodes, Turkey, Iraq, Iran and Spain. Sometimes stewing beef or lamb is added to the beans, sometimes garlic rather than onion is used, but all the recipes are variations on the same theme.

1 large onion, chopped	2 8-ounce cans tomato sauce
2 tablespoons olive oil	1 tablespoon chicken broth
½ cup sliced mushrooms	Juice from ½ lemon
3 pounds green beans, halved and ends removed	Salt and pepper to taste

Preheat the oven to 300°F.

In a large skillet, sauté the onion in the oil over medium-high heat until transparent, about 4 minutes. Add the mushrooms and sauté for 2 minutes more. Add the green beans and continue sautéing until the green beans are half cooked, about 8 minutes. Stir in the tomato sauce, broth, lemon juice and salt and pepper and cook for 3 minutes more to blend the flavors.

Transfer the green beans to a Pyrex baking dish with a lid. Cover and bake for 30 minutes. Serve hot.

Serves 6.

TURKEY
Spinach Balls

THIS IS ONE OF THE RECIPES GIVEN TO ME a long time ago by one of the mothers from Sephardic Hebrew Academy, now known as Maimonides Hebrew Academy, in Los Angeles. I cannot remember her name, though I can picture her fair skin and blond hair in my mind. She was from an old Turkish family. She invited me to her home, and we discussed food as our children played. Serve this recipe as a side dish or with rice as a main dish.

3 10-ounce bags fresh spinach	Salt and pepper to taste
2 large eggs	
¼ pound ground beef or turkey	Bread crumbs for dredging
2 pieces day-old good-quality white	Vegetable oil for frying
bread, soaked in 1 cup water	
and squeezed dry	

Wash the spinach leaves well. Remove the stems and chop the spinach finely. Steam for 5 minutes in a large heavy covered pot with about ½ inch of water in the bottom. Drain and squeeze out *all* the excess liquid. The spinach must be absolutely dry, or the balls will not hold together. If the spinach seems moist after squeezing out the liquid, return it to the dry pot and cook it without any water for a minute to ensure dryness. Place the spinach in a large bowl.

In a small bowl, lightly beat 1 of the eggs. Add the beaten egg along with the meat, bread and salt and pepper to the spinach. Knead the mixture well and shape into 12 balls.

Place the bread crumbs on a large plate and beat the remaining egg lightly in a shallow bowl. Roll the balls in the bread crumbs and then in the egg.

Pour about 3 inches of oil into a large skillet and heat to 350°F; a cube of bread tossed in will brown quickly. Add the spinach balls to the oil and fry, turning, until golden brown, about 3 to 4 minutes.

Remove with a slotted spoon and drain on paper towels. Serve immediately.

Makes 12 balls.

GREECE
Spinach with Beans

HE COMBINATION OF SPINACH AND BEANS is flavorful and nutritious. My stepmother, Ann Grau, has a great technique for removing dirt from spinach: first, plunge the spinach into hot water, and then immediately plunge it into cold water to revive it and free any hidden dirt or sand trapped in the leaves.

1 cup small dried black-eyed peas or small dried white beans (great Northern, flageolet or haricot beans)	1 tablespoon tomato paste
	3 cups beef broth
	2 garlic cloves, pressed
3 10-ounce bags fresh spinach	Juice from ½ lemon
3 tablespoons olive oil	Salt and pepper to taste

Soak the beans for 8 hours or overnight in enough water to cover.

Wash the spinach well, removing all dirt. Remove the stems and chop the spinach finely. Steam for 2 minutes in a large heavy covered pot until just wilted, then drain and set aside.

In a medium saucepan, combine the oil and tomato paste. Add the beef broth, beans and garlic and cook over medium heat for 30 minutes, or until the beans are soft. Stir in the spinach and cook for 10 minutes more. Season with the lemon juice and salt and pepper. Serve hot or at room temperature.

Serves 4 to 6.

INDIA

Cauliflower with Green Peas

OU CAN PLAY UP THE SPICES IN THIS SIMPLE BOMBAY DISH by adding some cayenne pepper and chopped fresh cilantro. Serve with white basmati rice.

¼ cup vegetable oil	Dash each of pepper, paprika
1 medium onion, chopped	and turmeric
1 garlic clove, minced	1 large cauliflower head,
1 tablespoon chopped fresh parsley	cut into florets
1 teaspoon salt	1½ cups fresh or frozen green peas
½ teaspoon curry powder	

In a large heavy pot with a lid, heat the oil and sauté the onion over medium-high heat until tender, about 4 minutes. Add the garlic, parsley, salt, curry powder, pepper, paprika and turmeric. Cook for 5 minutes to soften the garlic and blend the flavors, then add the cauliflower and peas.

Cover, reduce the heat to low and cook for 25 minutes, until cauliflower is tender. Serve hot.

Serves 4 to 6.

ITALY
Zucchini with Garlic and Lemon

MY FAMILY LIKES THIS SIMPLE PREPARATION of zucchini sautéed with garlic and dressed with lemon juice.

1	pound zucchini, thinly sliced		Juice from 1 lemon
3	tablespoons olive oil		Salt and pepper to taste
2	garlic cloves, minced	¼	cup finely chopped fresh parsley

Sprinkle the zucchini slices lightly with salt and set in a colander in the sink to drain for 20 minutes. Squeeze out the excess water.

Heat the olive oil in a nonstick pan over medium-high heat and add the garlic and zucchini. Sauté until the zucchini slices are golden and still somewhat firm. Transfer with a slotted spoon to a large bowl. Sprinkle with lemon juice, salt and pepper and parsley. Serve hot or cold.

Serves 4.

ITALY

Roasted Tomatoes

THESE SIMPLE YET FLAVORFUL TOMATOES make a versatile side dish.

1 cup finely chopped fresh parsley	10 plum tomatoes (Romas),
5 garlic cloves, minced	cut in half lengthwise
½ cup extra-virgin olive oil	Salt and pepper to taste

Preheat the oven to 350°F.

Mix together the parsley, garlic and olive oil. Using a teaspoon, hollow out the tomatoes and fill them with the parsley-garlic mixture. Sprinkle with salt and pepper and place them on a baking sheet.

Bake for 45 minutes, or until the tomatoes are soft. Serve at room temperature.

Makes 20 small roasted tomato halves.

IRAQ AND TURKEY
Okra in Tomato Sauce
(Bamyah)

BAMYAH, OR OKRA, IS A FAVORITE IN THE SEPHARDIC WORLD, though most cooks disagree on how best to cook it. My husband, Yacov, the in-house authority, prefers his okra fried first. When I serve him other versions, he tells me that the dish is not right, that the okra needs to be fried, "like my aunts make it, like my mother!"

2	pounds okra	2	tablespoons tomato paste
2	tablespoons white vinegar		Juice from 1 lemon
3	tablespoons olive oil	1	tablespoon sugar
2	garlic cloves, thinly sliced	1	teaspoon salt, or more to taste
1	28-ounce can peeled tomatoes, chopped	2	tablespoons fresh dill
½	cup water		Pepper to taste

Wash the okra and trim the stems without cutting into the vegetable. Place the okra in a medium bowl with the vinegar and enough hot water to cover. Set aside for ½ hour. Drain the okra in a colander and pat dry.

Heat the olive oil in a large skillet. Fry the okra over medium heat, turning, until golden, about 15 minutes. Remove from the skillet and set aside.

Add the garlic and tomatoes to the skillet and sauté for about 5 minutes. Add the water, reduce the heat to low and simmer for 15 minutes. Add the tomato paste, lemon juice, sugar and salt. Stir in the okra, cover and cook for 30 minutes, or until the okra is tender. Stir in the dill, add salt and pepper and serve.

Serves 6.

EGYPT
Egyptian Fried Potatoes
(Pommes de Terre Safrito)

THESE EGYPTIAN-STYLE FRENCH FRIES are usually prepared after baking a chicken or meat roast. The lemon juice adds a nice touch to the flavor.

6 potatoes, peeled or unpeeled	Juice from 1 lemon
¼ cup fat drippings from a roast or chicken, or olive oil	Salt to taste
2 garlic cloves, minced	1 tablespoon finely minced fresh cilantro (optional)

Cut the potatoes into wedges about 1 inch thick.

Heat the drippings or olive oil in a large skillet over medium-high heat. Add the potatoes and sauté for 5 minutes, tossing occasionally to prevent sticking. Cover the pan, reduce the heat to medium and cook for 10 minutes.

Add the garlic, increase the heat to medium-high and sauté for 3 minutes more, or until golden. Season with lemon juice. Drain on paper towels. Sprinkle with salt and cilantro, if using, and serve.

Serves 4.

Fried Leek and Potato Patties
(Kefte di Prasa)

THIS RECIPE FROM REBECCA LEVY IS WONDERFUL at Passover. Serve it as a vegetarian main dish or as a side dish.

6	large leeks, dark green ends removed, remainder sliced into 2-inch pieces	½	cup matzo meal
		1	teaspoon salt
1	large boiling potato, peeled	1	teaspoon pepper
2	garlic cloves, crushed	2	large eggs, lightly beaten

About 2 cups vegetable oil for frying

In a large pot, boil the leeks for 1 hour, or until they are so soft that they will disintegrate when squeezed. Remove from the heat and drain in a colander. When they are cool, squeeze out all the excess water; they must be dry.

In a small saucepan, boil the potato for 10 minutes, or until it is completely soft. Drain and mash.

In a mixing bowl, combine the leeks, mashed potato and garlic. Fold in the matzo meal and season with the salt and pepper. Add the eggs and mix.

Heat half the oil in a large skillet over medium-high heat. Form the leek mixture into patties the size of small hamburgers. If the mixture is too moist to form into patties, add a little more matzo meal and try again.

Fry the patties in batches, turning once, until golden on both sides, about 3 minutes per side. Add more oil to the skillet as needed. Drain the patties on paper towels and serve hot.

Makes 12 patties; serves 6.

Rice and Grains

Recipes

INDIA

Basmati Rice Pilaf

THIS COLORFUL AROMATIC RICE is often served as a side dish in the Jewish communities of Bombay and Cochin, in southwest India on the Arabian Sea.

2 cups basmati rice	½ teaspoon nutmeg
3 tablespoons vegetable oil	½ teaspoon salt
3 tablespoons minced onion	2 cups chicken broth
6 ounces mushrooms, sliced	½ teaspoon saffron threads soaked
2 whole cloves	in 2 tablespoons boiling water
1 1-inch piece cinnamon stick	½ cup slivered almonds

Wash the rice and soak it in cold water for 30 minutes. Drain in a colander.

Heat the oil in a medium skillet. Add the onion and cook over medium-high heat until tender, 3 to 4 minutes. Add the mushrooms and sauté until tender, about 5 minutes. Add the cloves, cinnamon stick, nutmeg and salt.

In a large saucepan, bring the chicken broth to a boil. Stir in the soaked saffron threads, the rice and the onion mixture. Bring to a boil, cover with a tight-fitting lid, reduce the heat to low and simmer until the rice is fully cooked, 25 to 30 minutes. Remove the cloves and cinnamon stick and sprinkle with the almonds before serving.

Serves 6.

Red Rice
(AROZ)

RED RICE, SERVED THROUGHOUT GREECE, Rhodes and Turkey, is preferred by many over white. Red rice is also served in Spain and Mexico; in fact, many of the settlers of Mexico were Sephardic Jewish refugees escaping the Spanish Inquisition during the 15th century.

2	cups long-grain white rice	1	teaspoon salt
2	tablespoons vegetable oil	2	cups water
1	cup tomato sauce		

Place the rice in a large bowl. Fill the bowl with cold water and then drain it off, repeating the process until the water runs clear.

In a large saucepan, heat the oil over medium-high heat. Add the rice and sauté for about 1 minute, until translucent. Add the tomato sauce, salt and water and bring to a boil over high heat. Reduce the heat to low, cover and simmer for 30 minutes, or until all the liquid has been absorbed. Fluff with a fork and serve.

Serves 6.

Egyptian Rice Pilaf

RICE IS TO THE EGYPTIANS WHAT COUSCOUS IS TO NORTH AFRICANS; it is served daily as a staple. This recipe produces an aromatic dish using *fideo* (a type of vermicelli pasta) and rice.

4	tablespoons vegetable oil (or butter if you are preparing a dairy meal)	2	cups long-grain white rice (basmati can be used)
1	medium onion, finely chopped	6	coriander seeds
1	garlic clove, crushed	½	teaspoon cinnamon
½	cup *fideo* or any vermicelli pasta	2½	cups chicken broth or water
			Salt to taste

In a large skillet, heat the oil or butter. Add the onion and garlic and cook over medium heat until transparent, about 4 minutes.

Crush the pasta between your fingers to break it into pieces about ¾ inch long. Add the pasta to the onion and garlic. Sauté over medium-high heat until golden brown, about 3 minutes.

Stir in the rice and cook until translucent, about 3 minutes. Add the coriander and cinnamon. Pour the broth or water over the rice. Season with salt.

Reduce the heat to low, cover and simmer until the rice is firm on the outside but tender to the bite, about 20 minutes, adding more water if the rice begins to stick to the pan. Fluff with a fork and serve.

Serves 4.

Persian Rice
(Chelo)

To an Iranian cook, the preparation of rice is an art, and every detail is open to discussion: the quality and brand of rice, the age of the grain, the length of the grain, the amount of time the rice must be soaked before steaming and the resulting color of the rice. The dish is well worth the added attention. At a festive event, the rice is mounded on a flat platter and garnished with various decorative ingredients. It is served with the *chelo*, a crust formed when some of the rice is allowed to stick to the bottom of the pan. The highly prized crisp *chelo* is sometimes presented on its own platter.

3 cups basmati rice	¼ cup vegetable oil
Salt	

Rinse the rice with cold water in a colander. Place the rice in a bowl and add cold water to cover and 1 teaspoon salt. Soak for at least 30 minutes and up to 5 hours, then drain in a colander.

Choose a pot with a tight-fitting lid. Fill the pot with 4 cups water and 2 teaspoons salt and bring to a boil. Stir in the rice, bring to a boil and boil for 5 minutes; the rice should be slightly soft but not fully cooked. Drain in a colander and set aside.

Add the oil to the same pot and heat over medium heat. Using a ladle, spoon the rice back into the pot, forming a cone shape, building the rice in the center of the pot away from the edges. Poke several holes in the mountain of rice to allow steam to rise freely from the bottom.

Cover the pot, first with a clean dish towel, then with the lid. Steam over very low heat for 30 minutes. Then, leaving a ½-inch layer of rice on the bottom of the pot, gently scoop out the steamed rice and set it aside. Cook the rice remaining in the pot over the very lowest heat with the lid ajar for about 30 minutes, until the rice forms a golden crust. Turn off the heat. Pour the steamed rice back into the pot, cover with the lid and allow the rice to stand for 15 minutes.

When you are ready to serve, carefully turn the whole pot over onto the serving plate. The rice should come out in the shape of a cake with the golden crust on top.

Serves 6.

IRAN

Rice with Barberries

YACOV'S COUSIN DORA THROWS GREAT PARTIES. I have to admit that her vision of what a party should be has stretched my sensibilities. The following recipe is just one of many rice platters to be served at a party. Dora usually serves rice with dill and broad beans, rice with orange zest and almonds, plain rice with yellow *chelo* (crust), and this dish, rice with barberries.

Barberries are small, raisinlike red berries that have a very tart taste; they are available in Middle Eastern specialty markets. In this recipe, they are sautéed with onion as a garnish.

¼	cup barberries	1	small onion, finely chopped
1	teaspoon salt	¼	teaspoon saffron threads soaked
2	cups basmati rice		in 2 tablespoons boiling water
3	tablespoons margarine or		
	vegetable oil		

Soak the barberries in ⅓ cup water for 30 minutes.

Rinse the rice with cold water in a colander until the water runs clear.

In a large nonstick pot with a tight-fitting lid, bring 5 cups water and the salt to a boil. Add the rice and boil for about 6 minutes, until the rice is partially cooked. Drain in a colander.

In the same pot, heat 2 tablespoons of the margarine or oil over medium heat. Spoon the rice back into the pot, forming a pyramid. Using the long handle of a wooden spoon, poke a couple of holes into the mound so that steam will circulate into the rice. Cover the pot, first with a clean dish towel, then with the lid. Reduce the heat to low and steam for 30 minutes.

In a separate saucepan, heat the remaining 1 tablespoon margarine or oil and sauté the onion over medium-high heat until golden, about 4 minutes. Drain the barberries and add them to the onion. Stir in the saffron mixture.

To serve, spoon the rice into a mound on a large platter and sprinkle the barberry mixture over the top.

Serves 6.

Iran
Rice with Dill and Baby Lima Beans

THIS POPULAR DISH COMBINES THE FLAVOR OF FRESH DILL with small lima beans and delicate long-grain basmati rice. It sometimes includes meat or potatoes, but I like this vegetarian version best. I enjoy eating it with thick whole-milk yogurt on the side.

2	cups basmati rice	¼	teaspoon saffron threads
1	10-ounce box frozen baby lima beans	8	tablespoons (1 stick) margarine, or ½ cup vegetable oil
1½	teaspoons salt	½-1	cup chopped fresh dill, stems removed
4	tablespoons hot water		

Wash the rice by rinsing it in cold water in a colander. Place in a bowl, add cold water to cover and soak for at least 2 hours.

In a 4-quart saucepan with a tight-fitting lid, bring 2 cups water to a boil. Add the rice, beans and 1 teaspoon of the salt. Boil, uncovered, for 7 minutes. Remove from the heat and drain in a colander. Rinse with lukewarm water.

In the same saucepan, place the hot water, saffron, butter or oil and the remaining ½ teaspoon salt. Return the pan to the stove and bring to a boil. Pour half of the mixture into a cup and set aside.

Combine the dill with the rice and beans. Spoon the rice back into the pot, forming a cone-like mound in the center of the pot. Using the long handle of a wooden spoon, make a deep hole in the center of the mound. Cover the pot, first with a clean dish towel, then with the lid, and cook over medium heat for 5 minutes. Remove the cover and sprinkle the reserved saffron mixture on top. Cover and steam over very low heat for 40 minutes.

To serve, turn the rice onto a serving plate and with a spatula gently remove the bottom crust and arrange it on top.

Serves 4 to 6.

Iraqi-Style Rice with Red Lentils
(Kitchree)

SINCE LENTILS AND BEANS ARE CONSIDERED "COMMON" FOOD, they are never served on Shabbat. I learned this lesson the hard way by serving *kitchree* to impress my husband's cousins, who were visiting from France.

Traditionally, *kitchree* is served on Thursdays as a dairy meal to accentuate the division between the splendor of Shabbat and the rest of the week. The combination of rice and lentils is soothing and nurturing, a complete meal in itself. The red lentils are small and delicate, and as they cook, they disintegrate into the rice. We serve this dish with *leben* (thick whole-milk yogurt) and garnish it with green olives.

1 cup small red lentils (found in Middle Eastern specialty markets and health-food stores)	1 8-ounce can tomato sauce
	1 teaspoon salt
	3 cups water
2 cups long-grain white rice, preferably basmati	4 garlic cloves, chopped
	2-4 tablespoons cumin
8 tablespoons (1 stick) margarine or butter	

Clean the lentils by rinsing them several times in cold water. Pick out any that are discolored and discard any small stones that may be mixed in. Cover the lentils with cold water and soak for 1 hour; drain.

Meanwhile, in a separate bowl, wash the rice. Rinse it several times with cold water until the water runs clear. Cover with cold water and set aside for 1 hour. Drain.

In a large nonstick pot, melt 4 tablespoons of the margarine or butter. Add the lentils, rice, tomato sauce, salt and water. Bring to a boil and stir once with a fork. Reduce the heat to low, cover and cook for 20 to 25 minutes, until all the liquid has been absorbed.

Sauté the garlic in the remaining 4 tablespoons margarine or butter in a small saucepan over medium heat until lightly golden, about 3 minutes. Stir in the cumin. When the rice and lentils have finished cooking, pour the garlic mixture over the top and gently stir. Continue cooking over low heat for another 10 minutes to distribute the flavors. Fluff with a fork and serve.

Serves 6.

SYRIA
Lentil and Rice Pilaf
(Mujeddara)

THIS VEGETARIAN DISH NEEDS ONLY A SALAD to be a complete meal. The brown lentils used are firmer than small red lentils and hold their shape throughout the cooking process.

2	cups brown lentils	2	cups long-grain white rice, washed
1	large onion, chopped	1½	teaspoons salt
4	tablespoons vegetable oil	⅛	teaspoon pepper
4	cups water	3	tablespoons pine nuts

Wash the lentils in cold water. Discard any that are discolored and any small stones that may be mixed in. Cover the lentils with cold water and soak for 2 hours; drain.

In a large heavy pot, sauté the onion in 3 tablespoons of the oil over medium-high heat until golden. Add the water along with the lentils, rice, salt and pepper. Bring to a boil, cover, reduce the heat to low and simmer for 30 minutes, or until all the water has been absorbed.

In a small skillet, sauté the pine nuts in the remaining 1 tablespoon oil over medium heat until lightly golden, about 3 minutes. Sprinkle the pine nuts over the rice and lentils before serving.

Serves 8.

Bulgur Pilaf

MY DAUGHTER, SATYA, LOVES THIS COMBINATION of bulgur wheat and tiny noodles. It is a nice change from rice or potatoes. Bulgur comes in three grinds: fine, medium and coarse. I prefer the coarse variety for this recipe because it is slightly chewy and offers a contrast to the delicate vermicelli.

½ cup pine nuts	1¼ cups coarse bulgur
3 tablespoons vegetable oil	2 cups chicken vegetable broth
1 onion, thinly sliced	½ cup water
½ cup vermicelli, broken into 1-inch pieces	Salt to taste

In a medium heavy saucepan, sauté the pine nuts in 1 tablespoon of the oil until golden, about 2 minutes; remove and set aside. Add the remaining 2 tablespoons oil and sauté the onion until golden, about 4 minutes; remove with a slotted spoon and set aside. Add the vermicelli and sauté until lightly golden, about 3 minutes, then add the bulgur, broth, water and salt and bring to a boil. Cover, reduce the heat to low and cook for 15 to 20 minutes, or until all the liquid has been absorbed.

Transfer the pilaf to a serving platter and top with the onion and pine nuts.

Serves 4.

Sweets

Recipes

✦

I R A N
Almond Cookies

HESE ALMOND COOKIES are not light and fluffy like some macaroons but rather rich and solid. I was served them often by my mother-in-law when I was nursing my children. She told me over and over again how much infants like the almonds, the sugar and the cardamom. She claimed that her cookies increase a mother's milk. Who knows? But they definitely pacified my nerves.

3 large egg yolks	1 tablespoon rose water (found in Middle Eastern and other specialty shops)
1 cup sugar	
1½ cups finely ground almonds	
3 teaspoons ground cardamom	Whole blanched almonds for decoration (optional)
1 teaspoon baking soda	
	1 egg yolk, beaten with a little water, for glaze

In a food processor fitted with the metal blade, blend all the ingredients except the whole almonds and egg yolk.

Preheat the oven to 300°F, with a rack in the middle. Line 2 cookie sheets with waxed paper.

Scoop out teaspoon-sized balls of dough and arrange them on the cookie sheets, leaving about 2 inches between them. Flatten each one slightly, using your palm. Press an almond into the top of each, then brush with the egg yolk mixture.

Bake until lightly golden, about 20 minutes. Cool on a rack.

Makes 36 cookies.

EGYPT

Sephardic Biscuits

(Kahke)

KAHKE, HARD BISCUITS SHAPED LIKE SMALL BAGELS or bracelets, are commonly served with coffee or tea. The flavor varies from one country to another, but they are never especially sweet. I prefer to make the dough in a food processor. One can also mix it in a bread machine or by hand in a mixing bowl, as it was traditionally done.

1 6-ounce fresh yeast cake	1 teaspoon salt
1 cup lukewarm water	8 tablespoons (1 stick) margarine or butter, melted
1 teaspoon sugar	
3½ cups all-purpose flour	1 egg, lightly beaten with a few drops of water, for glaze
1-2 teaspoons aniseeds	
1-2 teaspoons *mahlab* (a spice found in Middle Eastern shops), optional	Sesame seeds

Preheat the oven to 350°F, with a rack in the middle, and oil a baking sheet.

Dissolve the yeast cake in ½ cup of the lukewarm water in a small bowl and add the sugar. Let stand for 10 minutes, or until foamy.

Combine the flour, aniseeds, *mahlab*, if using, and salt in a food processor fitted with the metal blade and process, slowly adding the margarine or butter while mixing. Pour in the yeast mixture in a slow stream. Add the remaining ½ cup lukewarm water or enough to make a firm dough.

Break off walnut-sized pieces of dough and roll each between your hands to create 5-inch-long strands. Bring the 2 ends together and pinch them together to form a circle.

Using a pastry brush, brush the top of each piece with the egg mixture. Pour the sesame seeds into a shallow bowl. Dip the egg side of each piece into the sesame seeds. Place the biscuits on the baking sheet.

Bake for 20 minutes, then reduce the heat to 225°F and bake for 1 hour more, or until biscuits are hard. Cool on a rack. Leave the biscuits uncovered for 1 day, then store them in an airtight container or in reclosable bags.

Makes 2 dozen biscuits.

Sesame Seed Biscotti

(*Biscochos de Guevo*)

ISCOCHOS MEANS "TWICE-BAKED." These biscuits are first baked like cookies for 20 minutes, then stacked on their sides in a warm oven for several hours to dry out completely. The results are delicious. *Biscochos* will not become stale, for the additional drying time keeps them fresh longer. Rebecca Levy, who gave me the recipe, uses a mixture of Pillsbury All-Purpose flour and Better Bread flour.

3⅓ cups flour	**Topping**
1½ teaspoons baking powder	1 egg, beaten
Dash of cinnamon	¼ teaspoon sugar
3 extra-large eggs	Drop of vegetable oil
1 cup plus 2 tablespoons sugar	¼ cup sesame seeds, or ¼ cup
½ cup minus 1 tablespoon	sugar mixed with 1 teaspoon
vegetable oil	cinnamon
½ teaspoon vanilla extract	

Preheat the oven to 350°F, with a rack in the middle, and oil a baking sheet.

Mix the flour, baking powder and cinnamon in a medium bowl; set aside.

In a large mixing bowl, beat the eggs with an electric mixer until they are a creamy lemon color. Add the sugar and beat until smooth. Add the oil and beat again. Stir in the vanilla. With a wooden spoon, add the flour mixture little by little, mixing well. Let the dough rest for 10 to 15 minutes.

Meanwhile, make the topping: Combine the beaten egg with the sugar and oil.

Cut the dough into walnut-sized pieces. Roll each piece on a cutting board with the palms of your hands into 5-inch-long ropes (figure 1). Connect the 2 ends to form a circle (figure 2). Make small incisions with a sharp knife along the outer edge to create a wreath (figure 3).

Brush the top of each wreath with the egg mixture, then dip into the sesame seeds or the cinnamon mixture (figure 4).

Place the *biscochos* on the baking sheet. Bake for 20 minutes, then remove from the oven. Reduce oven heat to the lowest setting, about 150°F. Balance the *biscochos* on their sides in a baking pan, return them to the warm oven and bake for 2 to 3 hours. Cool on a rack. Leave the *biscochos* uncovered for 1 day, then store in airtight containers.

Makes about 36 biscochos.

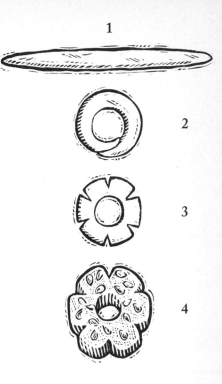

TUNISIAN BISCOTTI
(Boulou)

SIMILAR TO A EUROPEAN MANDEL BREAD or Italian biscotti, *boulou* is dense-textured, sweet and laced with chocolate, nuts, raisins and orange essence. The mother of my friend Evelyne Guez taught a group of us this recipe one memorable afternoon, pointing out that it is as much work to bake one loaf as it is to bake four. You can freeze the extra loaves or give them to friends or divide the recipe to make less.

Served with tea or coffee, this sweet biscuit is a luscious treat.

6 extra-large eggs, plus 1 egg yolk for glaze	8½ teaspoons finely grated orange zest
2 cups sugar	7½-8 cups all-purpose flour
2 teaspoons orange-blossom water (found in Middle Eastern and other specialty shops), optional	½ cup golden raisins
	½ cup pine nuts
	½ cup unsalted pistachios
4½ teaspoons baking powder	3 ounces bittersweet chocolate, chopped
1½ cups vegetable oil	Whole blanched almonds and
1½ teaspoons ground fennel seeds	sesame seeds for decoration

Beat the 6 eggs in a large bowl with an electric mixer until they are a creamy yellow color. Slowly beat in the sugar, orange-blossom water (if using), baking powder, oil, fennel and orange zest. With a wooden spoon, fold in 7½ cups flour, a little at a time, stirring by hand.

Turn out the dough onto a bread board and knead. The dough should not be too sticky; if necessary, add more flour. Knead until the dough is heavy and smooth, then roll it into a ball. Place in a bowl and cover with a clean dish towel. Let rest for 1 hour.

Preheat the oven to 375°F, with a rack in the middle, and oil 2 baking sheets.

Cut the dough into 4 sections. Roll each section out into a rough rectangle with a rolling pin, adding more flour if necessary.

Working with one section at a time, cover two-thirds of the dough with raisins, pine nuts and pistachios. Cover the remaining third of the dough with the chocolate. Roll up into a jelly roll, starting from the chocolate side. Gently press, removing any air, pinching the edges together and pressing in the ends. Repeat the process with the remaining 3 sections.

Brush the top of each loaf with the yolk glaze. Decorate the top with 2 rows of almonds and a sprinkling of sesame seeds.

Bake, checking the bread after 30 minutes, for approximately 45 minutes, until the loaves are golden. Cool on a rack before slicing them ½ inch thick on the diagonal. Wrap the extra loaves in aluminum foil and freeze.

Makes 4 loaves.

RHODES
Tahini Cookies
(Kurabie)

THESE COOKIES ARE SHAPED LIKE SMALL MOUNDS and decorated with a nut pressed into the top of each. The combination of cloves and tahini gives the cookies an exotic flavor. They are a big success with my kids.

1 cup vegetable oil	½ teaspoon cloves
1 cup sugar	2-2½ cups all-purpose flour
1 tablespoon tahini (sesame seed paste)	1 large egg, lightly beaten
2 teaspoons almond extract	About 24 whole blanched almonds for decoration
1 teaspoon cinnamon	

Preheat the oven to 300°F, with a rack in the middle.

Combine the oil, sugar, tahini, almond extract, cinnamon and cloves in a food processor fitted with the metal blade or in a large mixing bowl. Add 2 cups of the flour and process, or stir it in gradually with a wooden spoon. If the dough is shiny, it needs more flour. Continue to add the flour a few tablespoons at a time until the dough is firm but pliable.

Pinch off small pieces of dough. Roll each piece into a ball about 2 inches in diameter. Stick a nut in the top of the ball, then very lightly dip the top into the beaten egg to cover it with just a thin film. Place the balls on a cookie sheet, spacing them about 1 inch apart.

Bake for 10 minutes, then rotate the pan from back to front, move the rack to the upper half of the oven and bake for another 10 minutes, then rotate the pan again.

Bake until lightly golden but not brown, about 5 minutes more. Remove from the oven. Cool on a rack. Do not touch the cookies until they are completely cool. Store in airtight containers.

Makes about 2 dozen cookies.

IRAQ
Nut Cookies
(Haji Baddah)

RECEIVED THIS RECIPE from Tina Rahamin of Canada. Mrs. Rahamin is a perfect example of an Iraqi Jewish mother. Once as I was departing for Los Angeles, she met me in the Toronto airport with two large parcels, asking if I would deliver them to her daughter. She gave me careful instructions on how to hold the packages and keep them away from the heat and told me to call Annette immediately upon landing to let her know the packages had arrived. After delivering them, I asked my friend what her mother had sent that was so important. Cookies, of course—about eight dozen!

Haji baddah is a delicious lacy cookie that is a perfect Passover treat, as it contains no flour.

3	extra-large egg whites	1	cup coarsely ground almonds
¼	teaspoon cream of tartar	1	teaspoon vanilla powder
¾	cup sugar		(found in Middle Eastern shops)
2	cups coarsely ground walnuts		

Preheat the oven to 325°F, with a rack in the middle.

Beat the egg whites with an electric mixer until stiff but not dry. Fold in the cream of tartar. Slowly fold in the sugar. Fold in the nuts and the vanilla powder.

Using a tablespoon, spoon the mixture onto a nonstick cookie sheet. Bake for 15 minutes, or until the cookies are lightly golden. Do not remove the cookies from the cookie sheet until they are completely cool. Store in airtight containers.

Makes 36 cookies.

TUNISIA

Haman's Ears

(Dablah)

HE NAME OF THIS COOKIE consigns the recipe to Purim, a festive Jewish holiday that is celebrated to commemorate Queen Esther's success in undoing a plot to destroy the Jewish people in ancient Persia. In the story, Haman was the wicked advisor to the king. It is a traditional custom to eradicate Haman by making and eating food named after him: cookies in the shape of his ears, pasta named after his hair and round foods called "Haman's eyes." The most common kinds of food involve his ears. This recipe was given to me by my friend Evelyne Guez.

4	large eggs	2	tablespoons sugar
	Pinch of salt		
1½	cups all-purpose flour		Vegetable oil for deep-frying
1	cup fine semolina		Honey Syrup (see page 221) or
⅓	cup finely ground walnuts		confectioners' sugar

Beat the eggs and salt with an electric mixer until they are a creamy lemon color. Mix in the flour and semolina with a wooden spoon.

In a small bowl, combine the walnuts and sugar; set aside.

Roll the dough out on a lightly floured surface until it is about ⅛ inch thick. Cut the dough into 2-inch squares and place ½ teaspoon filling in the center of each. Fold 1 corner of the square over the filling to form a triangle. Pinch the edges to seal well.

Pour about 3 inches of oil into a deep pot and heat to 350°F; a cube of bread tossed in will brown quickly. Drop the triangles into the oil one by one until the pot is filled; do not crowd.

When the pastries are golden, remove them with a slotted spoon and place them on paper towels to drain.

To serve, dip into the honey syrup or confectioners' sugar. Serve at once.

Makes about 3 dozen cookies.

TUNISIA

Honey Syrup

THIS IS A SWEET SYRUP used for dipping pastries and cookies. It can be made ahead of time and refrigerated; reheat it before using.

2 cups sugar	1 strip orange peel (from about
2 cups water	¼ medium orange)
Juice from ½ lemon	3 tablespoons honey

Put 3 tablespoons of the sugar into a medium saucepan. Heat over very low heat, stirring, until the sugar melts and caramelizes, 3 to 5 minutes. When the desired color is reached, add the water and stir; be careful, as the mixture will spatter. Add the remaining sugar, lemon juice and orange peel. Simmer for 20 minutes. Add the honey, reduce the heat to low and simmer for an additional 20 minutes, stirring occasionally. Remove the orange peel. Let cool for a few minutes before using.

Makes 1½ cups syrup.

IRAQ
Date-Filled Biscuits

MY MOTHER-IN-LAW ALWAYS SERVED TEA or Turkish coffee in the afternoon to revive us from the traditional midday nap. Often she would have visitors, friends who came to have their coffee cups read. Claire was a master coffee-cup reader. Her readings were often quite accurate, and she had a following of ladies who believed in her talent.

This system of fortune-telling is very popular throughout Sephardic culture. First, you are served a demitasse of very strong Turkish coffee. After you have drunk all the liquid and only the fine moist powder of coffee remains, you quickly invert the cup onto its saucer. After a couple of minutes, the reader picks up the cup and, from the images she sees in the coffee granules on the sides of the cup, foretells events.

To accompany the afternoon tea or Turkish coffee, my mother-in-law would serve an assortment of homemade cookies, including this Iraqi specialty. These flat golden disks are filled with a thin layer of sweet date paste and topped with sesame seeds.

Filling

1   pound pitted dates, or a 13-ounce package pressed pitted dates
1   tablespoon margarine or butter
½   cup orange marmalade (optional)
1   cup finely chopped walnuts (optional)
1   teaspoon cinnamon

Dough

1   teaspoon active dry yeast
1   cup warm water
    Pinch of sugar
4   cups all-purpose flour
1   teaspoon aniseeds (optional)
½   teaspoon salt
8   tablespoons (1 stick) margarine or butter
¼   cup vegetable oil

1 egg yolk, mixed with a little water, for glaze	Sesame seeds

To make the filling: If using ordinary pitted dates, cut them in half. Put them in a medium saucepan with enough water to cover. Cook over low heat, stirring occasionally, for 30 minutes. Drain off the excess water and add the margarine or butter, marmalade and walnuts (if using) and cinnamon. If using the pressed dates, place all the ingredients in a medium saucepan and stir over low heat for several minutes, just enough to blend into a smooth paste. Set aside to cool.

Preheat the oven to 350°F, with a rack in the middle.

To make the dough: In a cup, combine the yeast and warm water. Add the sugar and let stand for 15 minutes, or until foamy. In a large bowl or a food processor fitted with the metal blade, combine the flour, aniseeds (if using) and salt. With a fork or pastry blender or in the food processor, cut the margarine or butter into the dry ingredients. Add the oil. Add water, a little at a time, while processing or mix it in with a fork to make a firm dough. Set aside for 1 hour.

Pinch off a small ball of dough. With a rolling pin on a clean surface, roll out a circle about 3 inches in diameter. Place a heaping teaspoon of filling in the center and fold the dough over it from all sides, pressing the edges together to form a stuffed little cookie. Use your hands to flatten the cookie into a disk. Repeat until all the dough and filling have been used. Turn the cookies over and brush the smooth side with the egg-yolk mixture. Sprinkle sesame seeds lightly over the top. Using a toothpick, poke 5 small holes in the top of each cookie to encourage it to flatten as it cooks.

Bake on an ungreased cookie sheet for about 20 minutes, or until the bottoms are golden. Cool on a rack. Store in airtight containers.

Makes 36 cookies.

SYRIA
Nut-Filled Cookies
(Ma'amoul)

MY FRIEND HUGETTE GALANTE says the secret ingredient in these cookies is Wondra flour. It makes a light, crumbly dough that melts in your mouth. Hugette decorates her cookies using a special Israeli wooden cookie press. I use a fork, which works just fine. You can also fill these cookies with date filling (see page 222).

Dough	**Filling**
2 cups all-purpose flour	1 cup walnuts or pistachios
1 cup cake flour	½ cup sugar
1 cup sugar	2 tablespoons orange-blossom water
1 teaspoon baking powder	(found in Middle Eastern
8 tablespoons (1 stick) margarine	and other specialty shops)
or unsalted butter, at room	
temperature	Sifted confectioners' sugar
6-8 teaspoons water	

To make the dough: Preheat the oven to 350°F, with a rack in the middle. In a food processor fitted with the metal blade, mix together the flours, sugar, baking powder, margarine or butter and 6 teaspoons of the water. The dough should be firm but malleable; add up to 2 teaspoons more water if necessary. Remove the dough from the food processor and set it aside in a bowl. Wipe out the food processor.

To make the filling: Combine all the ingredients in the food processor and process until crumbly.

Pinch off pieces of dough the size of walnuts. Roll them into a ball. Insert your thumb into the center of each ball, pushing slightly to create a hollow. Fill the hole with the filling and pinch the opening closed. Place the balls on a cookie sheet. Press down the tops of the cookies with the tines of a fork.

Bake for about 20 minutes, or until the cookies are lightly golden; do not brown. Cool them on a rack, then roll them in confectioners' sugar and serve. Store in an airtight container.

Makes about 3 dozen cookies.

TUNISIA
Finger Cookies

THIS RECIPE WAS GIVEN TO ME BY MY FRIEND Donna Cohen, who received it from a Tunisian friend's mother visiting from France. We had a lively time translating it from French, then converting the grams into cups and spoonfuls. The result is a delicious sweet vanilla cookie with just a touch of orange essence. You can turn this recipe into an Iraqi-style cookie by replacing the orange zest with ground cardamom and substituting rose water for the orange-blossom water. This cookie is the perfect accompaniment to an afternoon cup of coffee.

4 large eggs	1 tablespoon orange-blossom water (found in Middle Eastern and other specialty shops)
1 cup sugar	
1 package (5/16 ounce) vanilla sugar (found in Middle Eastern shops)	1 cup vegetable oil
1 tablespoon finely grated orange zest	5 cups all-purpose flour
	3 tablespoons baking powder

In a large mixing bowl, beat together the eggs, sugar and vanilla sugar with an electric mixer until the mixture is a creamy lemon color. Stir in the orange zest, orange-blossom water and oil.

In a small bowl, combine the flour and baking powder. With a wooden spoon, fold the flour into the egg mixture, 1 cup at a time, until a firm but pliable dough is formed.

Line 2 cookie sheets with aluminum foil. Preheat the oven to 350°F, with a rack in the middle.

Divide the dough into 36 balls and roll each ball into a 4-to-5-inch cylinder. Set the cylinders side by side (but not touching) on the baking sheet. Bake for 15 minutes, or until lightly golden. Cool on a rack. Store in an airtight container.

Makes 36 cookies.

GREECE
Semolina Cake

HEN I WAS 18, I camped my way across England to France and down through Spain, Italy, Greece and Turkey. While on the island of Corfu, I contracted German measles and had to stay inside my tent for a week. A kind Greek lady who ran the campground brought me a semolina cake. The following recipe reminds me of that long-ago treat.

Traditionally, semolina cake is served on Shabbat afternoon.

Cake
- 8 tablespoons (1 stick) margarine or butter
- ¾ cup sugar
- Grated zest from 1 lemon
- 3 large eggs
- 1½ cups fine semolina
- 1 cup all-purpose flour
- 4 teaspoons baking powder
- ½ cup milk
- Blanched almonds for decoration

Syrup
- 3 cups water
- 2½ cups sugar
- 3 tablespoons lemon juice

Preheat the oven to 350°F, with a rack in the middle. Grease a 9-x-13-inch baking dish.

To make the cake: Cream the margarine or butter, sugar and lemon zest with an electric mixer until light and fluffy. Add the eggs one at a time, beating to incorporate each.

Combine the semolina, flour and baking powder in a small bowl. Fold into the butter mixture. Stir in the milk. Pour the batter into the baking dish. Decorate the top with even rows of almonds.

Bake for 45 minutes, or until the cake is golden and a tester inserted in the middle comes out clean. Cool on a rack.

Meanwhile, make the syrup: In a medium saucepan, heat the water over medium-high heat. Add the sugar and stir until it is dissolved. Add the lemon juice and bring to a boil. Reduce the heat to medium and cook, without stirring, for 20 minutes. Remove from the heat and let cool.

Prick the surface of the hot cake with a toothpick or skewer and pour 1 cup of the cooled syrup over the cake. Leave the cake in the pan until it has cooled, then cut it into square or diamond shapes. Any extra syrup can be refrigerated for use at another time.

S e r v e s 1 0.

Honey Nut Cake
(Tishpishti)

THE FACT THAT THIS CAKE CONTAINS NUTS AND EGGS instead of flour makes it especially suitable for Passover, but it is so good that it is served year-round.

Cake

6	large eggs, separated
½	cup sugar
½	teaspoon vanilla extract
1	teaspoon water
1½	teaspoons baking soda
1	teaspoon cinnamon
½	teaspoon allspice

2	cups finely ground hazelnuts (filberts) or walnuts
	Zest from 1 orange
	Zest from 1 lemon

Syrup

¾	cup honey
¼	cup water
1	teaspoon lemon juice

Preheat the oven to 350°F, with a rack in the middle. Grease a 9-x-13-inch baking pan.

To make the cake: Beat the egg yolks with an electric mixer until they are a creamy lemon color. Slowly beat in the sugar. Continue beating until the mixture is smooth and the sugar has been incorporated. With a wooden spoon, stir in the vanilla, water, baking soda, cinnamon, allspice, nuts and grated citrus zest.

In a separate bowl, beat the egg whites until stiff peaks form. Fold the egg whites into the yolk mixture. Pour into the baking pan and bake for 30 minutes, or until golden on top and a tester inserted in the middle comes out clean. Cool on a rack.

Meanwhile, make the syrup: In a small saucepan, combine the honey, water and lemon juice and bring to a boil. Remove from the heat and let cool.

Poke tiny holes in the surface of the hot cake with toothpicks and pour the syrup over the cake. After the syrup has been absorbed, cut into squares.

Serves 8.

TUNISIA

Nut Sponge Cake

EVELYNE GUEZ WAS THRILLED WHEN HER TUNISIAN AUNT, Fridah Boublil, gave her this wonderful recipe for a Passover cake after years of holding out. The recipe gives you a choice of nuts. Blanched almonds make an elegant cake. Almonds with skins, hazelnuts or walnuts produce a more earthy cake. Select only one kind of nut per recipe. The art of making this cake is in the preparation of the nuts, which should be chopped fine—into a powder—in a food processor or blender.

8 large eggs, separated	1 teaspoon orange-blossom water
½ teaspoon salt	(found in Middle Eastern
¾ cup sugar	and other specialty shops)
½ pound nuts (blanched or	1 teaspoon almond extract
unblanched almonds, hazelnuts	
or walnuts), finely chopped	
1 teaspoon grated orange zest	

Preheat the oven to 300°F, with a rack in the middle.

Line a 9-inch round or 8-x-8-x-2-inch square baking dish with aluminum foil.

In a medium bowl, beat the egg whites and salt with an electric mixer until stiff but not dry. Set aside in the refrigerator.

In a large bowl, beat the egg yolks and sugar with an electric mixer until smooth. Mix in the nuts, orange zest, orange-blossom water and almond extract with a spatula.

Slowly fold the egg whites into the yolk mixture with a rubber spatula, just enough to blend. Do not overmix.

Pour the batter into the baking dish. Bake for 45 minutes, or until the cake is lightly golden. Turn the oven off and leave the cake in the oven for 10 minutes more, then cool the cake on a rack.

To serve, run a knife around the edge of the cooled cake and remove it from the pan, then remove the foil and cut the cake into cubes.

Serves 10.

IRAQ
Spiral Pastries

THESE SWEET PASTRIES ARE POPULAR in many of the Middle Eastern countries. Sometimes brightly colored, they vary in flavor from country to country. I like the ones flavored with rose-water syrup. I received this recipe from Yacov's aunt.

Syrup

3 cups sugar

1½ cups water

2 tablespoons rose water or orange-blossom water (found in Middle Eastern and other specialty shops)

Batter

1 package (2¼ teaspoons) active dry yeast

2 cups lukewarm water

1 teaspoon sugar

2¼ cups all-purpose flour
    Pinch of salt

1 tablespoon vegetable oil, plus more for frying

To make the syrup: Combine the sugar and water in a medium saucepan. Bring to a boil, stirring, then reduce the heat to low and simmer, without stirring, until the syrup thickens. Stir in the rose water or orange-blossom water and simmer for 2 minutes more. Remove from the heat and let cool.

To make the batter: Dissolve the yeast in the lukewarm water. Add the sugar and let stand for 10 minutes, or until foamy. Combine the flour and salt in a large bowl. Slowly add the yeast mixture and 1 tablespoon oil to the flour while mixing.

Pour at least 3 inches of oil into a deep pot and heat to 375°F; a cube of bread tossed in will brown quickly. Pour the batter into a pastry bag or a plastic squirt bottle, such as an empty mustard or ketchup bottle. Squeeze the batter into the hot oil, swirling the batter to create a coiled pastry 4 to 6 inches in diameter. Turn the pastry over immediately so that the batter becomes golden brown on both sides. Remove with a slotted spoon and gently place on paper towels to drain. Pour the syrup onto a deep plate. While the pastries are still warm, dip them, one at a time, into the syrup. Repeat, cooking and dipping the pastries, until all the batter has been used.

Makes about 2 dozen pastries.

GREECE
Shredded Filo Pastry
(Kadayfi)

ONE OF MY FAVORITE TIMES OF DAY in the Middle East is around 4 P.M., when one revives oneself from the afternoon nap with a strong cup of Turkish coffee and sweets. The following pastry, *kadayfi*, is popular throughout the Middle East. It consists of shredded filo dough, which becomes light and delicate when baked, and a filling mixture of nuts and spices. The pastry is saturated with a sweet syrup flavored with aromatic flower essence.

Filling

2 cups coarsely chopped walnuts
or pistachios

1 teaspoon cinnamon

¼ teaspoon cloves

Pastry

1 16-ounce package shredded filo
dough, also known as *knafa*
(found in Middle Eastern shops)

8 tablespoons (1 stick) margarine
or butter, melted

Syrup

3 cups sugar

2 tablespoons lemon juice

1½ cups water

1 teaspoon rose water
(found in Middle Eastern
and other specialty shops)

Preheat the oven to 350°F, with a rack in the middle. Grease a 9-x-13-inch baking pan.

To make the filling: In a small bowl, combine the walnuts, cinnamon and cloves.

To make the pastry: Pull the *knafa* gently to loosen it. Spread half of the shredded filo dough in the baking pan. Top it with the walnut mixture and half of the melted margarine or butter. Spread the remaining filo and the remaining margarine or butter over the walnut mixture.

Bake for 30 to 40 minutes. Cool on a rack.

Meanwhile, make the syrup: Combine the sugar, lemon juice and water in a saucepan. Bring to a boil over medium heat, stirring constantly. Once the sugar has dissolved and the mixture is boiling, do not stir. Reduce the heat to low and simmer for 10 to 15 minutes. Remove from the heat and stir in the rose water.

Pour half of the syrup evenly over the hot pastry. Wait 10 minutes to allow the pastry to absorb the syrup, then pour on the remaining syrup.

Make diagonal slices in one direction across the pan, then in the opposite direction, to make diamond shapes. Let stand in the pan for 3 to 5 hours at room temperature before serving.

Serves 8 to 10.

IRAQ
NUT-FILLED FILO ROLLS

THESE NUT-FILLED COOKIES RESEMBLE BAKLAVA in flavor and texture. They are a little more work because of the rolling, but they are much easier to pick up and eat, making them a better choice for serving at a party. They are served piled high on platters and eaten with Turkish coffee or tea.

Syrup

¾ cup honey

¾ cup sugar

¾ cup water

2 tablespoons lemon juice

1 tablespoon rose water (optional)

Filling

4 cups finely chopped walnuts

1 cup sugar

1 teaspoon cinnamon

½ teaspoon allspice

Pastry

1 16-ounce package filo dough

1 cup (2 sticks) margarine or butter, melted

Preheat the oven to 350°F and lightly grease 2 cookie sheets.

To make the syrup: In a medium saucepan, combine the honey, sugar, lemon juice and water and bring to a boil, stirring, then reduce the heat to low and simmer, without stirring, for 15 minutes. Set aside and allow to cool. Stir the rose water, if using, into the cooled syrup.

To make the filling: Combine all the ingredients, mix well and set aside.

To make the pastry: Cut the filo stack in half lengthwise, then in half again (figure 1). Work

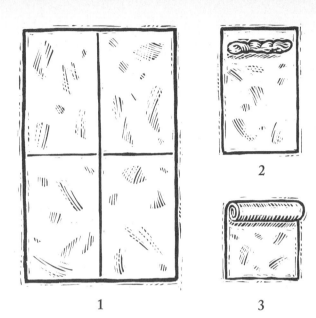

1   2   3

with 2 sheets at a time, covering the remaining sheets with a damp dish towel so that they do not dry out.

With a pastry brush, lightly brush 1 sheet with melted margarine or butter. Place another sheet of filo on top of the first and brush it with butter. Place 1 teaspoon filling at the end of the sheet (figure 2). Carefully roll up the pastry sheet from the filling end to make a small cigar-shaped pastry (figure 3). Repeat, using 2 filo sheets per pastry, until all the pastry sheets are used and there is no more filling. Place the pastries on the cookie sheets and bake for 20 minutes, until lightly golden.

Before serving, pour a little syrup over each pastry roll. Refrigerate any remaining syrup to be used at another time. Serve the pastries at room temperature.

Makes 60 pastries.

TURKEY
Baklava

I RECEIVED THE RECIPE FOR THIS BEST-KNOWN MIDDLE EASTERN CLASSIC from my friend Eileen Halpern, who was raised in a large Sephardic community in Seattle.

Syrup

1 cup sugar
1 cup water
⅓ cup honey
1 tablespoon lemon juice
1 tablespoon grated orange zest

Filling

3 cups coarsely chopped walnuts, pistachios or almonds
¼ cup sugar
½ teaspoon cinnamon
⅛ teaspoon cardamom

Pastry

1 16-ounce package filo dough
1 cup (2 sticks) margarine or butter, melted

Preheat the oven to 350°F, with a rack in the middle. Grease a 9-x-13-inch baking pan.

To make the syrup: Combine all the ingredients and bring to a boil, stirring. Reduce the heat to low and simmer, without stirring, for 15 minutes. The syrup can be made ahead of time and refrigerated. Reheat it before pouring over the pastry.

To make the filling: In a large bowl, combine all the ingredients, mix well and set aside.

To make the pastry: Place 1 sheet of filo on the baking pan. With a pastry brush, spread a thin layer of melted margarine or butter on the sheet. Cover with 2 more sheets of filo, brushing each with the margarine or butter. Sprinkle the top sheet with one-third of the filling, spreading it evenly over the surface. Add another layer of 3 filo sheets, brushing each sheet with margarine or butter. Sprinkle with another third of the filling. Repeat until all the filling is used, reserving 3 filo sheets for the final layer. Brush with margarine or butter.

Bake for 30 minutes, or until the pastry is golden brown. Remove from the oven and let cool on a rack for 10 minutes.

Cut diagonal slices in one direction, then in the other direction, to make diamond-shaped pieces. Pour the honey syrup over the warm pastry. Let cool and serve.

Makes 18 pastries.

TUNISIA
Tunisian Fried Chanukah Pastries
(Yo-Yos)

Y o-Yos, RESEMBLING DOUGHNUTS, are made during the holiday of Chanukah. If they are made during Passover, matzo meal is substituted for the flour. My friend Serge Cohen, who was born in Tunisia but spent his early adulthood in France as a chef, gave me the recipe for these wonderful treats.

Pastry

4 large eggs

¼ cup sugar

1 tablespoon vegetable oil, plus more for frying

4½ cups all-purpose flour

2 teaspoons baking powder

1 package (⁵⁄₁₆ ounce) vanilla sugar (found in Middle Eastern shops)

1 teaspoon orange-blossom water

1 teaspoon grated orange zest

Honey Syrup (page 221)

Beat together the eggs, sugar and the 1 tablespoon oil in a medium bowl with an electric mixer until creamy. In a large mixing bowl, combine the flour and baking powder. Fold the egg mixture into the flour with a wooden spoon. Add the vanilla sugar, orange-blossom water and orange zest.

Combine the ingredients until the consistency is slightly sticky; the batter should not crumble or fall apart, nor should it stick to your fingers when you work with it. If it is too sticky, gradually add more flour. If the batter is too dry, add a little more oil.

Turn the dough out onto a bread board and knead for a few minutes to create a smooth dough. Form it into a large ball, cover with a clean dish towel and set aside to rest for 30 minutes.

Roll the dough into small balls 2 inches in diameter. Work the balls into rings, poking a hole in the center of each. They should look like mini-doughnuts.

Pour 4 inches of oil into a deep pot and heat to 350°F; a cube of bread tossed in will brown quickly. Fry the doughnuts in the oil until golden brown, turning once. Remove them from the oil with a slotted spoon and drain on paper towels. Dip them into the honey syrup. Serve immediately, stacked on a large platter.

Makes 30 pastries.

ITALY
Chanukah Fritters
(Frittelle di Chanukah)

DURING THE EIGHT NIGHTS OF CHANUKAH, families join together lighting candles, spinning dreidels and eating fried foods to commemorate a miracle. A small renegade Jewish army called the Maccabees won a battle against the mighty Syrian army, which was occupying Jerusalem. When the Jews returned to the holy Temple, they found it had been desecrated and there was no pure oil to light the menorah. A small amount of oil was finally found, enough to last for only one night, but it burned for eight nights, allowing time for new sacred oil to be created.

I was given this recipe by a friend whose mother is from Italy. Serving these little fried pastries flavored with aniseeds and raisins at Chanukah was their family's tradition.

Fritters			Vegetable oil for frying
2	envelopes active dry yeast		
1	cup lukewarm water		**Glaze**
3	cups all-purpose flour	1½	cups honey
2	teaspoons aniseeds	2	tablespoons lemon juice
1	teaspoon salt		
2	tablespoons vegetable oil		
1	cup raisins		

To make the fritters: Dissolve the yeast in the lukewarm water and let stand until foamy, about 5 minutes. Combine the flour, aniseeds and salt in a large bowl. Slowly add the yeast mixture and the oil. Mix with a wooden spoon until a dough is formed, then turn out onto a work surface and knead until the dough is smooth and elastic. Sprinkle the raisins over the dough and knead them in. Return the dough to a clean bowl, cover with a clean dish towel and let rise in a warm place until the dough doubles in bulk, about 1 hour.

Turn the dough out onto the work surface and flatten it until it is about ½ inch thick. Let it rest, uncovered, for about 15 minutes. With a sharp knife, cut it into 36 diamonds.

Pour at least 3 inches of oil into a deep pot. Heat the oil to 350°F; a cube of bread tossed in will brown quickly. Fry the diamonds several at a time, turning so that they are golden on both sides. Remove with a slotted spoon and drain on paper towels.

To make the glaze: Heat the honey and lemon juice in a small saucepan and boil for 3 minutes.

Arrange the fritters on a serving plate and drizzle the hot honey mixture over them. Serve immediately.

Makes 36 fritters.

MOROCCO

Dates and Prunes Stuffed with Marzipan

MOROCCANS LOVE COLOR AND SWEETS; this popular dessert made with home-made marzipan provides both. The recipe was given to me by my friend Nicole Halfon.

Marzipan
1 pound blanched almonds
1¼ cups water
1½ cups sugar
Juice from ½ lemon

2 pounds mixed dates and prunes
Food coloring, 3 colors (optional)
Honey Syrup (page 221) or
  Moroccan Dessert Syrup
  (page 248)

To make the marzipan: Soak the almonds for 30 minutes in cold water; drain and pat dry. Process in a food processor fitted with the metal blade or a nut grinder until they are finely ground.

Heat the water over medium-high heat and add the sugar. Cook, stirring, until the sugar dissolves and the mixture becomes frothy. Stir it into the almonds; add the lemon juice. Process in the food processor until the dough becomes thick and sticky. Set aside to cool.

If colored marzipan is desired, divide the marzipan into 3 balls. Add several drops of food coloring to each one, using a different color for each ball.

To assemble the stuffed fruits: Make a slit in the side of each date and prune and remove the pit.

Break off little pieces of marzipan and form each into a little ball slightly larger than the cavity left by the removed date or prune pit. Stuff the dates and prunes with the filling, allowing the marzipan to bulge out slightly.

To serve, dip the marzipan side of each fruit into warm syrup. Arrange on a serving platter with an assortment of other sweets.

Makes 2 pounds marzipan-stuffed fruit.

MOROCCAN DESSERT SYRUP

MAKE THIS SYRUP AHEAD OF TIME AND KEEP IT in your refrigerator for pouring over pastries. Reheat it before using.

2 cups confectioners' sugar	1½ tablespoons cornstarch
2 cups water	Juice from ½ lemon
½ cup fruit syrup (found in Middle Eastern or health-food shops)	½ teaspoon orange-blossom water

Combine the sugar and water in a medium saucepan and bring to a boil, stirring. Reduce the heat to low and simmer, without stirring, until the mixture has thickened slightly, about 10 minutes.

Add the fruit syrup and cook over very low heat for 30 minutes more, stirring often, until the mixture has thickened.

Combine the cornstarch and lemon juice in a small bowl and add to the syrup. Cook for 2 to 3 minutes, stirring. Remove from the heat and stir in the orange-blossom water. Store, covered, in the refrigerator for up to 1 month.

Makes 1-1¼ cups syrup.

IRAQ
Sesame Candy

IN IRAQ, SESAME CANDY IS SERVED PILED HIGH on decorative platters, usually accompanying other sweets for festive celebrations. I include it in my children's school lunches as an alternative to granola bars and fruit roll-ups.

2½ cups sesame seeds	¾ cup honey
1 cup chopped blanched almonds	½ cup sugar
¼ cup all-purpose flour	1 teaspoon lemon juice

Preheat the oven to 350°F. Grease a cookie sheet.

Combine the sesame seeds, almonds and flour in a medium bowl. Pour the mixture onto the cookie sheet and bake for 8 to 10 minutes, until lightly browned. Set aside.

In a medium saucepan, combine the honey, sugar and lemon juice. Bring to a boil over medium-high heat, stirring, then reduce the heat to medium and cook, without stirring, for 25 to 30 minutes, until the mixture reaches the soft-ball stage (a small amount dropped into a cup of ice water will form a soft, pliable ball), about 242°F on a candy thermometer.

Add the sesame seed mixture to the syrup. Cook over low heat for 5 minutes more, stirring occasionally. Remove from the heat and let cool for 2 minutes.

Turn the mixture out onto a wet wooden board. With wet hands, roll the mixture into a ball, then roll it into a ½-inch-thick cylinder. Press down several times to make the cylinder into a square log. Cut into slices and shape each slice into a diamond or a rectangle. Let cool until firm. Store in an airtight container, with the layers separated by waxed paper.

Makes 48 pieces.

TURKEY

Rosa's Marzipan
(Masapan)

THE MOTHER OF MY SISTER-IN-LAW CHAYA, Rosa Behor Levy, makes exquisite marzipan. Rosa is originally from Turkey but traces her lineage back to the Sephardic expulsion from Spain.

Every time Chaya and her husband visit us in the United States, her mother sends a large box of marzipan for my family. This is her recipe.

3	cups whole blanched almonds	½	cup light corn syrup
2	large egg whites		Juice from ½ lemon
		1	teaspoon vanilla extract or almond extract
2	cups sugar		
1	cup water		

Grind the nuts in a food processor fitted with the metal blade until they are as fine as powder. Transfer to a large mixing bowl. Beat the egg whites with an electric mixer until they are stiff but not dry and fold them into the ground almonds. Set aside.

In a medium saucepan, combine all the remaining ingredients. Bring the mixture to a boil, stirring, then reduce the heat to low and simmer, without stirring, for 20 minutes, or until it is thick and golden in color. Pour the syrup into the almond mixture and return it to the food processor. Blend until it becomes a smooth paste. Refrigerate the marzipan overnight.

The next day, roll the marzipan into walnut-sized balls. Allow to air-dry for several days before storing in an airtight container.

Makes approximately 2 pounds.

MIDDLE EAST
Tahini Paste Candy
(Halvah)

WHEN I WAS A CHILD, my father used to buy us halvah candy bars after our ritual deli dinner on Sunset Boulevard in Los Angeles. I had no knowledge of the Middle East or Israel at that time, and I did not associate the candy with any cultural lineage that I might have. I do remember being fascinated by the flavor and texture, which was like frozen ice cream without the cold.

2 cups sugar	1 16-ounce jar tahini (sesame seed paste), room temperature
1 cup water	2 egg whites
2 teaspoons vanilla extract	1 cup sliced unsalted almonds or pistachios

Bring the sugar and water to a boil, stirring. Reduce the heat to medium and cook, without stirring, until thick, 15 to 20 minutes. Remove from the heat and let cool slightly. Stir in the vanilla extract.

With an electric mixer, beat the tahini in a large bowl until smooth and creamy. In a separate clean bowl, beat the egg whites until stiff but not dry. Gently fold them into the tahini. Slowly fold in half the sugar syrup with a wooden spoon. Fold in the nuts and add the remaining syrup. Stir.

Transfer the mixture to a small nonstick loaf pan or cake pan. Cover with plastic. Let stand at room temperature and unmold after 3 days. Cut into wedges or squares. Store in the refrigerator for up to 1 month or in an airtight container.

Makes 1 loaf.

Sauces
and Condiments

Recipes

Garlic Sauce

(Azada)

AZADA, ALSO KNOWN AS SKORDALIA, is the Greek version of aioli, a smooth-textured garlic sauce that resembles a thick mayonnaise. It is served with fish or chicken. *Azada* is most easily prepared in a food processor or blender. Make sure that all the ingredients are at room temperature when you begin. Just as in the preparation of mayonnaise, the oil must be added very slowly in a steady stream so that it emulsifies; otherwise, the sauce will "break" and curdle. If you are whisking the oil in by hand, always stir in the same clockwise or counterclockwise direction. Because the eggs in this sauce are raw, make sure they are very fresh.

2 slices day-old good-quality white bread	1 cup extra-virgin olive oil
12 garlic cloves, peeled	1 cup vegetable oil
2 large egg yolks	Juice from 1 lemon
	Salt and white pepper to taste

Remove the crusts from the bread and soak in water for about 10 minutes. Squeeze all the water out of the bread.

Place the bread, garlic and egg yolks in a food processor fitted with the metal blade and process until smooth. Stir together the 2 kinds of oil in a cup with a pouring spout. While the processor is running slowly, add the oil in a thin stream. Add the lemon juice. Season with salt and white pepper. Refrigerate and serve cold. The sauce will keep in the refrigerator for several days.

Makes about 2½ cups.

YEMEN
Yemenite Hot Sauce
(Zhoug)

Y EMENITE CONDIMENTS ARE VERY SPICY and are added to many dishes; they are believed to ward off disease and give long life. This sauce is eaten with flatbreads or added to sauces and soups. In Israel, hot sauces like this one are called *harif*. They are often served as an accompaniment to falafel and added to almost any dish to increase the bite.

6 medium green chili peppers (jalapeño or serrano)	2 tablespoons olive oil
1 cup chopped fresh parsley	1 teaspoon salt
1 cup chopped fresh cilantro	1 teaspoon pepper
4 garlic cloves	1 teaspoon cumin

Puree the chilies in a blender or a food processor fitted with the metal blade. Add the parsley, cilantro and garlic. Add the olive oil and seasonings and blend again. Pour the mixture into a glass jar and refrigerate. *Zhoug* will remain fresh for up to 2 weeks.

Makes about 1½ cups.

INDIA

Fresh Cilantro-Mint Chutney

I FIRST DISCOVERED THIS CHUTNEY IN AN INDIAN RESTAURANT in Egypt with my husband in 1981. I requested the recipe immediately, and I have since eaten this very traditional chutney in many Indian homes and restaurants. It is simple to make and a lovely accompaniment to samosas and pakoras.

¼	cup lemon juice	½	cup finely chopped onion
2	tablespoons water	1-2	teaspoons seeded and chopped green chili pepper
1	cup fresh cilantro leaves, tightly packed	1	teaspoon salt
1	cup fresh mint leaves, tightly packed	¼	teaspoon pepper

Combine all the ingredients in a food processor fitted with the metal blade. Process until the mixture is perfectly smooth. Serve immediately with Indian Vegetable Fritters (page 41).

Makes about 1½ cups.

INDIA
Yogurt with Cucumbers and Tomatoes
(Raita)

IMAKE THIS SMOOTH, SOOTHING DISH to accompany rice and lentil dishes or vegetarian meals. Versions of it are enjoyed throughout the Middle East.

2 medium cucumbers, peeled and cut into ½-inch pieces	2 tablespoons finely chopped fresh cilantro
1 tablespoon finely chopped onion	2 cups plain yogurt
1 tablespoon salt	1 teaspoon cumin
2 tomatoes, cut into ½-inch cubes	

Mix the cucumbers, onion and salt in a small bowl. Let stand for 5 minutes. Squeeze the mixture with your hands to remove the excess moisture; transfer it to a medium bowl.

Add the tomatoes and cilantro. Mix together the yogurt and cumin in a small bowl and add to the vegetables. Gently toss, then refrigerate for 1 hour. Serve chilled.

Makes 3 cups.

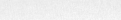

IRAN

Persian Fresh Herbs

(Sabzi Khordan)

HERBS ARE A QUINTESSENTIAL ELEMENT OF PERSIAN CUISINE, cooked into stews and egg dishes and also offered fresh within the same meal. The following herbs are served as an accompaniment to most Persian dishes. Traditionally, they are chilled and placed on a large communal platter with flatbread and raw walnuts and brought out before the main meal. The proportions should be to taste.

6 whole radishes, green tops left on	1 bunch fresh basil leaves
6 whole green onions, roots and ends trimmed, tops left on	1 bunch fresh tarragon leaves
1 bunch fresh spearmint leaves	6 walnuts for garnish

Wash all the herbs well, removing any dirt and stems. Pat dry with paper towels or use a salad spinner to remove the excess water. To serve, arrange the herbs on a platter and sprinkle with walnuts. Serve chilled.

Serves 6 to 10.

GREECE
Sweet Passover Condiment
(Haroset)

HAROSET IS SERVED DURING THE PASSOVER SEDER to symbolize the mortar used in Egypt when the Jews were slaves before their Exodus. Every Sephardic country has a unique combination of fruits, nuts and wine that is used in this holiday dish; the combination also varies from one family to another. The following recipes were given to me by a woman who had spent part of her life in Greece and part in Rhodes.

1¼ cups finely chopped dates	½ cup finely chopped walnuts
¾ cup finely chopped dried currants	3 tablespoons honey
¾ cup finely chopped dark raisins	¼-½ cup sweet red wine
½ cup finely chopped almonds	

Soak the dates, currants and raisins overnight in water to cover.

Transfer the mixture to a medium saucepan and cook in the soaking water until the fruit is soft, about 15 minutes. Drain and mash the fruit, adding the nuts and honey. Pour in the sweet wine until the mixture is thick, smooth and moist. Stir well and chill.

Makes about 3 cups.

RHODES

VARIATION

Haroset

1 medium orange	¼ cup sweet red wine, or more
1¼ cups finely chopped dates	as needed
½ cup honey or sugar	½ cup finely chopped almonds
Cinnamon and cloves to taste	

Peel and seed the orange and cut it into pieces. Blend or process the orange pieces and dates into a paste.

In a medium saucepan, combine the fruit paste and honey and simmer for 20 minutes, or until it thickens. Add the cinnamon and cloves and sweet wine. Simmer until very thick. Remove from the heat and stir in the nuts.

Makes about 2 cups.

IRAQ
Date Syrup
(Halek)

THIS SYRUP, THE CALCUTTAN VERSION of *haroset*, is also served in Iraq. My mother-in-law worked for days prior to Passover, producing huge pots full of a syrup similar to this one. Everyone in the family waited for the holiday with great anticipation. She made extra bottles for family members to take home.

6 cups pitted dates	15 cups water

Place the dates and water in a large pot and bring to a boil. As soon as the water boils, remove the pot from the heat and set aside for 3 hours; do not stir.

Line a large pot with a triple layer of cheesecloth. Pour 1 cup of the date mixture into the cheesecloth. Lift the 4 corners of the cloth and twist, squeezing the liquid into the pot. Twist and squeeze until all the liquid has been removed. Discard the date pulp. Repeat the process with another cup of the date mixture until all of it has been used.

Place the date-liquid pot on the stove and bring to a boil. Skim the scum off the surface so that the syrup is dark and clear. Reduce the heat to low and simmer for 40 minutes to 1 hour, until the liquid is reduced to less than half.

When the date syrup has cooled, pour it into a glass jar and refrigerate. It will keep for up to 2 months.

Makes 4 cups.

Menus

Moroccan Shabbat Evening Menu

Moroccan Carrot Salad, page 21
Tomato and Pepper Salad, page 22
Moroccan Eggplant Salad, page 28
Pita Bread, page 51

Baked Fish with Chickpeas, page 112

Moroccan Couscous, page 96
or
Chicken with Olives, page 119

Fresh Fruit
Almond Cookies, page 209
Dates and Prunes Stuffed with Marzipan, page 246

Sweet Mint Tea and/or Turkish Coffee

Tunisian Shabbat Afternoon Menu

Roasted Nuts: Cashews, Almonds, Chickpeas
Boukha (a liqueur made from figs)

Eggplant and Pepper Salad, page 25
Cooked Vegetable Salad, page 29
Anise, Fennel or Dill Root Salad, page 35
Pita Bread, page 51

Fish *H'raimi*, page 109

Spicy Beef Stew with White Beans *(T'fina Camounia)*, page 152

Fresh Fruit
Tunisian Biscotti *(Boulou)*, page 214, or Finger Cookies, page 226
Nut Sponge Cake, page 232

Turkish Coffee

Iraqi Shabbat Brunch/Lunch

Fried Eggplant Salad, page 26
Cooked Vegetable Salad, page 29
Brown Roasted Eggs, page 120
Green Olives
Pickled Turnips (available in Middle Eastern shops)
Pickled Mangos (available in Middle Eastern shops)

Pita Bread, page 51, or Yemenite Flatbread *(Melawach)*, page 56

Turnovers Stuffed with Chickpea Filling *(Sembussak)*, pages 62-63

Chicken Stuffed with Rice *(T'bit)*, page 120

Date-Filled Biscuits, page 222
Nut Cookies *(Haji Baddah)*, page 218, or Baklava, page 240
Fresh Fruit
Turkish Coffee

Syrian Festive Dinner

Tabbouleh (Bulgur Salad), page 36
Tahina, page 38
Hummus, page 39
Eggplant and Tahini Dip *(Baba Ghanoush)*, page 40
Fried Bulgur Dumplings with Meat Filling *(Kibbe)*, page 44
Pita Bread, page 51

Chicken with Potatoes *(Maaoude B'tata)*, page 124
Squash Stuffed with Rice and Meat *(Mersche)*, page 154

Fresh Fruit
Dried Fruits: Apricots, Dates, Prunes, Figs
Nuts: Almonds, Pistachios, Walnuts
Nut-Filled Cookies *(Ma'amoul)*, page 224
Turkish Coffee

Rhodian Festive Brunch/Lunch

Greek (or Turkish) Salad, page 30
Stuffed Grape Leaves *(Dolmas)*, page 42
Cheese-Filled Pastries *(Boyo de Queso)*, page 46
Savory Turnovers *(Borekas)*, page 64
Savory Stuffed Yeast Pastries *(Bolemas)*, page 66

Baked Fish in Tomato Sauce *(Peskado kon Salsa de Tomat)*, page 108
Red Rice *(Aroz)*, page 194

Sesame Seed Biscotti *(Biscochos de Guevo)*, page 212
Tahini Cookies *(Kurabie)*, page 216
Turkish Coffee

Iranian Festive Menu

Persian Fresh Herbs *(Sabzi Khordan)*, page 258

Herb-Stuffed Fish, page 110

Chicken in Walnut and Pomegranate Sauce *(Fesenjan)*, page 130
Green Vegetable Stew with Beef *(Qormeh Sabzi)*, page 138
Chopped Lamb Kebabs *(Shefta)*, page 140
Rice with Barberries, page 198
Rice with Dill and Baby Lima Beans, page 200

Almond Cookies, page 209
Spiral Pastries, page 234

Fresh Fruit
Dried Fruit
Nuts
Turkish Coffee

Vegetarian Menu I

Tabbouleh (Bulgur Salad), page 36

Stuffed Grape Leaves *(Dolmas)*, page 42
Tahina, page 38
Hummus, page 39
Pita Bread, page 51

Eggplants Stuffed with Chickpeas and Mint, page 176
or
Syrian Sour Soup *(Hamud)*, page 82, served with
Red Rice *(Aroz)*, page 194
or
Lentil and Rice Pilaf *(Mujeddara)*, page 204, served with
Yogurt with Cucumbers and Tomatoes *(Raita)*, page 257

Nut-Filled Filo Rolls, page 238
Dates and Prunes Stuffed with Marzipan, page 246
Fresh Fruit
Turkish Coffee

Vegetarian Menu II

Moroccan Carrot Salad, page 21
Tomato and Pepper Salad, page 22
Fried Eggplant Salad, page 26
Turnip Salad, page 34, or Anise, Fennel or Dill Root Salad, page 35
Pita Bread, page 51

Cheese-Filled Pastries *(Boyo de Queso)*, page 46
Turnovers Stuffed with Chickpea Filling *(Sembussak)*, page 63
Savory Stuffed Yeast Pastries *(Bolemas)*, page 66
Fried Pastries with Potato Filling *(Brik)*, page 68

Sephardic Biscuits *(Kahke)*, page 210
Nut Cookies *(Haji Baddah)*, page 218
Baklava, page 240
Fresh Fruit

Indian Menu

Indian Vegetable Fritters *(Pakoras)*, page 41
Deep-Fried Vegetable Pastries *(Samosas)*, page 70
Fresh Cilantro-Mint Chutney, page 256
Indian Flatbread *(Naan)*, page 58

Baked Fish with Coriander, page 104
Chicken Curry Stew, page 127, or Chicken and Chickpea Stew *(Meetha)*, page 131
Cauliflower with Green Peas, page 183
Basmati Rice Pilaf, page 193

Spiral Pastries, page 234
Jasmine Tea

Jewish Holidays

Rosh Hashanah

MEANING "HEAD OF THE YEAR" IN HEBREW, Rosh Hashanah, the Jewish New Year, is celebrated on the first two days of Tishrei (September-October). This is not a time of rejoicing but rather of introspection and dedication to the newness of the coming year, a time to commit to new goals and new directions. The holiday is celebrated by eating sweet foods to symbolize the sweetness of the new year. Other foods are also consumed to signify new choices. Pomegranates with their 613 seeds are symbolic of the righteous deeds one should perform during the year. The head of a fish is served to remind us that it is better to be a head than a tail and to remind us to be aware at all times.

Yom Kippur

The Day of Atonement, Yom Kippur, is the most solemn celebration in the Jewish tradition. It falls 10 days after Rosh Hashanah and is the culmination of 10 days of penitence. On this day, all adults (people over the age of 13) abstain from all sensory worldly pleasures, including eating, drinking, wearing perfume, jewelry or leather and having sexual relations. Additionally, it has the same prohibitions as Shabbat, when one is not allowed to create, drive or kindle a flame. The day is spent in prayer, asking for forgiveness for transgressions, and is followed by a breaking-of-the-fast celebration.

Sukkot

Sukkot, the Feast of the Tabernacles, which falls on the 15th day of Tishrei (three days after Yom Kippur) and lasts for eight days, commemorates the time the Israelites spent in the desert after leaving Egypt. This joyous celebration requires the building of a *sukkah*, a temporary dwelling that is a bit like a tent with a palm-branch roof (one must be able to see the stars through the roof). In Newport Beach, California, or in Paris, France, structures are created in backyards, on balconies and in parking lots, just as they were in Israel. The idea is to feel as if one is in the desert.

The *sukkah* is decorated with fruits and flowers. A bouquet of a single palm branch, a willow branch and a myrtle branch, and a citron known as an *etrog* are used to bless the dwelling. All meals are served in the *sukkah* during the week. In some Orthodox traditions, the family actually sleeps in the *sukkah*. This is a fun holiday, when friends and family get together to eat in each other's temporary dwellings. There is always a bit of competition about who has built the best *sukkah*.

Simchat Torah

Simchat Torah, "happiness of the law," is celebrated the day after Sukkot ends, the 23rd day of Tishrei. It honors the completion of the reading of the Torah, the book of laws, which has 54 sections, one of which is read each week. It also inaugurates the beginning of the new cycle of readings. This day is celebrated by drinking liqueur and eating candies, and there is much singing and dancing.

Chanukah

This holiday commemorates the purification of the temple in Jerusalem after the victory of the Maccabees over Antiochus Epiphanes, who prohibited the Jews from practicing their religion in an effort to assimilate them into Greek culture. A renegade Jewish army revolted, recapturing the holy temple. They found enough oil to keep the temple menorah lit for one day, but it burned for eight days, signifying a miracle. To commemorate the miracle, Jewish families light a menorah for eight days at the end of Kislev (November-December). It is customary to eat fried foods and to make charitable gifts.

Tu B'shevat

My youngest child, Claire, calls this holiday the "birthday of the trees." It is a celebration of the reawakening of nature after winter on the 15th day of Shevat (January-February), with tables adorned with fresh and dried fruits, nuts and flowers.

Purim

The 15th day of Adar (February-March) is a joyful celebration of the pious Jewish woman Esther, who was chosen because of her beauty to marry King Ahasueros of Persia. The king's wicked advisor, Haman, plotted to annihilate the Jewish people, and Esther, upon learning of the plan, set out to win the king's favor by preparing feasts for him. In the end, she saved her people from destruction. This holiday is celebrated by feasting, drinking and gift-giving.

Pesach (Passover)

Celebrated on the 15th to the 22nd of Nisan (March-April), Pesach commemorates the Exodus of the Jews from Egypt. They left in such haste that there was no time for the bread to rise, so they had only unleavened bread. To celebrate the holiday correctly is an arduous process, for all rooms and clothing must be thoroughly cleaned to remove *hametz* (leavening).

Shavuot

Originally celebrated at the end of the harvest season on the sixth day of Sivan (May-June), Shavuot is celebrated with dairy meals. At the time of the Temple, this holiday was observed as the second of three annual "pilgrim festivals," when offerings of the first fruits of the summer harvest were taken to Jerusalem.

Tisha B'av

The saddest day on the Jewish calendar, Tisha B'av falls on the ninth day of Av (July-August). It commemorates times when misfortune has befallen the Jewish people: the destruction of the temple in Jerusalem, the death of great spiritual leaders, the expulsion from Spain and many pogroms. Before this day, it is customary to eat lentil stew and hard-boiled eggs. On the day itself, a strict fast is observed. Tisha B'av is regarded as a highly superstitious day, especially in the Sephardic communities.

To Order Products by Mail

Sultan's Delight
P.O. Box 090302
Brooklyn, NY 11209
(800) 852-5046
(718) 745-2563
Fax (718) 745-2563
www.sultansdelight.com

Index